TWELVE GREAT MODERNISTS

BOOKS BY
LAWRENCE F. ABBOTT

———◆———

Impressions of Theodore Roosevelt
Letters of Archie Butt
Twelve Great Modernists

TWELVE GREAT MODERNISTS

HERODOTUS	THOMAS JEFFERSON	BEETHOVEN
ST. FRANCIS	JOHN MARSHALL	EMERSON
ERASMUS	FRANÇOIS MILLET	DARWIN
VOLTAIRE	GEORGE STEPHENSON	PASTEUR

By
LAWRENCE F. ABBOTT

NEW YORK
DOUBLEDAY, PAGE & COMPANY
1927

4194

TO

W. B. A.

IN GRATEFUL APPRECIATION OF
HER SYMPATHETIC HELP WITH-
OUT WHICH THIS BOOK COULD
NEVER HAVE BEEN WRITTEN

CONTENTS

PRAESCRIPTUM

THOSE readers who may expect theological controversy in these pages will be disappointed. The word modernist is not used here in its current and technical ecclesiastical sense. I have taken the liberty of giving this often acrimoniously discussed word a broader meaning—or rather, I have gone back to the original meaning found in its Latin root, *modus* or manner. When we say that a man is a modernist we ought to be referring to his mode or manner of thinking and not to his theories or creeds. This, at least, is the sense in which the title of this book is chosen.

The modernist believes in life, in progress, in spiritual and intellectual evolution, rather than in tradition and dogma; in the republic of reason rather than the despotism of creeds. He refuses to live in the past, although he gladly gets light from the past to illuminate and make clearer the path toward the future. The conflict between the traditionalist (or, to use the jargon of the day, the fundamentalist) and the modernist is not a new thing, nor is it confined to theology.

It is as old as recorded literature and is found in the domains of law, art, poetry, music, history, pedagogy, and science, as will appear, I hope, in the biographical sketches that compose this volume.

These sketches are not the fruit of original research. They make no pretense to scholarship. In writing them no original documents have been consulted and no lost manuscripts have been discovered. Their purpose is merely to pass on, if possible, to the general reader like myself some of the pleasure which the reading of biography has given me for now nearly fifty years.

Not having the talent, patience, or application of the scientific student I like to take my history in biographical doses. Biography—good biography, that is—has the entertaining qualities of fiction, the encyclopedic qualities of political history, and the inspiring qualities of devotional literature. "From the records of men whose passage through life has been marked by rays of shining light," said Pasteur, "let us piously preserve every word and deed, no matter how slight, that may reveal the sources of their inspiration for the education of posterity." He might well have added for our own education as well.

The notion of attempting such a book as is here offered was put into my mind some fifteen years ago by reading Andrew D. White's *Seven Great Statesmen*, a model work of its kind, readable and rereadable. I cannot and do not hope to compare my sketches to his profound yet lively studies. That would be presumptuous, for Dr. White was one of the foremost historical scholars of our time. But I plead, in justification of my venture, the dictum of Thomas Carlyle which Dr. White prints as a motto facing his title page: "Great men, taken up in any way, are profitable company."

The men I have elected to take up here have interested me not only because of their achievements, but because of their spirit of courage and progress. All of them were denounced by some of their contemporaries as dangerous radicals and innovators. It is not this, however, that makes them modernists. The true modernist, since he believes in the life of the spirit, has reverence for the great spirits of the past, and, more than all, for that Great Spirit which most of us cannot define but which all of us can see working in the long history of mankind and which has been called so happily by Matthew Arnold "the Power not ourselves which makes for righteousness."

This spirit of reverence for the true, the beautiful, and the good appears in striking form in most of the dozen modernists who have especially interested me; I think it may be discovered in all of them—even in Herodotus and Voltaire.

LAWRENCE F. ABBOTT.

CORNWALL, NEW YORK
October 1st, 1926

HERODOTUS

THE TRAVELLER

TWELVE GREAT MODERNISTS

ONE: HERODOTUS

THE TRAVELLER
BORN 484 B. C.—DIED 424 B. C.

O F ALL the ancients Herodotus was the most
modern. He was a small-town man. It
might almost be said that he was a Main Street
man. For, although a Greek in culture, temperament, and language, he was born in the insignificant, provincial city of Halicarnassus (now
Boodroon), in Asia Minor, of which we should
think little or nothing to-day if it had not been
his birthplace.

Halicarnassus was on the southeastern shore
of the Ægean Sea, within easy access of Athens
by galley or trireme, almost in sight of the islands
of the Grecian archipelago. As a boy, nearly
half a millennium before the birth of Christ,
Herodotus must often have wondered about the
marvels of the Greek capital just as the Main
Street boy wonders about the skyscrapers of

Chicago or New York. For Phidias was at that very time planning and carving the Parthenon, a building whose miraculous and stately beauty is still talked of throughout the world. If it is thought to be extravagant to speak of Herodotus, for centuries a favourite companion of men of letters and culture, as a Main Street product, I appeal to Lord Macaulay who, whatever may be thought of his merits as a scientific historian, is undeniably a great stylist and critic. In one of his enjoyable essays Macaulay says:

> The faults of Herodotus are the faults of a simple and imaginative mind. Children and servants are remarkably Herodotean in their style of narration. They tell everything dramatically. Their *says hes* and *says shes* are proverbial. Every person who has had to settle their disputes knows that, even when they have no intention to deceive, their reports of conversation always require to be carefully sifted. If an educated man were giving an account of the late change of administration, he would say,—"Lord Goderich resigned; and the King, in consequence, sent for the Duke of Wellington." A porter tells the story as if he had been hid behind the curtains of the royal bed at Windsor: "So Lord Goderich says, 'I cannot manage this business; I must go out.' So the King says,— says he, 'Well, then, I must send for the Duke of Wellington,—that's all.'" This is the very manner of the Father of History.

We do not have to take Macaulay's word alone to sustain the conception of Herodotus as a

small-town man—that is to say, a man who is
naïf, unsophisticated, and like a child in the
simple integrity of his mind. Herodotus himself supplies the materials for such an estimate
of his character. Constant allusions and comments in his book show that he was childlike and
superstitious, although manifestly sincere, in his
religious convictions. The mixture of credulity
and reason in his beliefs—which ought not to
be surprising when we consider the age in which
he lived—appears in his account of some small
winged snakes which he describes as living in
certain trees in Arabia.

The Arabians say that the whole world would swarm
with these serpents if they were not kept in check in the
way in which I know that vipers are. Of a truth Divine
Providence does appear to be, as one might expect before-
hand, a wise contriver. For timid animals which are a
prey to others are all made to produce young abundantly,
so that the species may not be entirely eaten up and lost;
while savage and noxious creatures are made very unfruit-
ful. The hare, for instance, which is hunted alike by
beasts, birds, and men, breeds so abundantly as even to
superfœtate, a thing which is true of no other animal.
You find in a hare's belly, at one and the same time, some
of the young all covered with fur, others quite naked,
others again just fully formed in the womb, while the hare,
perhaps, has lately conceived afresh. The lioness, on the
other hand, which is one of the strongest and boldest of
brutes, brings forth young but once in her lifetime, and
then a single cub; she cannot possibly conceive again

since she loses her womb at the same time she drops her young.

This is certainly not the science of natural history at its best, but it leads to the fair inference that Herodotus believed in a Power above nature which directs and controls the affairs of mankind. Like Moses, however, he regarded and feared this celestial or olympian power as a "jealous God." Says Canon Rawlinson, whose translation and interpretation of Herodotus is a fine flower of English scholarship: '

The οθόνος (jealousy) of God is a leading feature in Herodotus's conception of the Deity, and no doubt is one of the chief moral conclusions which he drew from his own survey of human events and intended to impress upon us by his history. . . . The idea of an avenging God is *included* in the Herodotean conception, but it is far from being the whole of it. Prosperity, not pride, eminence, not arrogance, provokes him. He does not like anyone to be great or happy but himself. What is most remarkable is that, with such a conception of the Divine Nature, Herodotus could maintain such a placid, cheerful, child-like temper. Possibly he was serene because he felt secure in his mediocrity.

By his use of the word mediocrity I suppose that Canon Rawlinson alludes to Herodotus's social and political position—to his small-townishness, so to speak—perhaps even to his financial standing, for he was a man of moderate

means, although he must have spent large sums
in his long journeys and voyages. His literary
work and his travels were not, however, the
avocations of a man of wealth and leisure, but
were turned into a source of income, for he gave
public readings from his history, and it is said
that the Athenian assembly voted him a payment of ten talents (more than ten thousand
dollars of our money) for his success as a public
entertainer. Thus his mediocrity was clearly
not intellectual, for he had the genius not only
to create the first prose narrative style in the
history of Western literature, but, in modern
fashion like Dickens, Thackeray, and Mark
Twain, to transmute it into gold on the lecture
platform.

Like many popular writers who strike out on
a new path, Herodotus has been savagely attacked, his arch-critic being the moralist Plutarch. The admirers of Herodotus and of Plutarch, both of whom deserve all the admiration
that has been given them, have tried to reconcile
the almost malignant attacks of the former by
calling the bitter criticisms of Plutarch apocryphal and ascribing them to the interpolations of
a "pseudo-Plutarch." The best opinion, however, considers most of these alleged apocryphal
writings as genuine and they must therefore

stand, not as a reflection upon Herodotus but upon the prejudice and partiality of Plutarch himself, in spite of his good morals.

By Cicero and other admirers, Herodotus has been called the Father of History; by Plutarch and other detractors, the Father of Lies. Partisans of the school of Thucydides take issue with Cicero; all fair-minded men who can discriminate between fiction and falsehood take issue with Plutarch. I will avoid becoming involved in the conflict by offering another appellation. Herodotus may very well be called the Father of Tourists. In this respect he is decidedly a modernist, for touring is a very modern habit. It is true that Moses and his people were great travellers in their day nearly a thousand years, it is alleged, before the days of Herodotus; but they travelled as the beasts of the field travel— to escape death and destruction; or, as our Puritan fathers braved the Atlantic, in search of religious freedom. Nothing of this sort prompted Herodotus to make his unprecedented journeying. He travelled for the fun of the thing and to record his impressions of the lands and peoples and folklore that he happened upon. Someone may criticize my use of the phrase "unprecedented journeying" and refer to Odysseus as the earliest and greatest of ancient travellers. But

Odysseus was a figment of the imagination, a character in a great poetical novel, like the figures in Chaucer's *Canterbury Tales*, while Herodotus was a very real person who took himself, and deserves to be taken, seriously. He would not have compared himself, I think, nor are we to compare him with Thucydides, who was a statesman and not a humanist, and whose "style," to quote Macaulay again, "is weighty, condensed, antithetical, and not infrequently obscure." A juster comparison would be with Marco Polo the Italian, or Ibn Batuta the Mohammedan, of whom one penetrated Asia in the Thirteenth and the other encircled Africa in the Fourteenth Century and left picturesque accounts of their adventures.

That Herodotus is to be regarded as a traveller, an observer, rather than a historian was the opinion of one of the most competent critics of the Eighteenth Century. In America we know Thomas Gray, fellow of Pembroke Hall, Cambridge University, as a poet and as the author of merely one poem at that—the famous Elegy. But a contemporary who knew him well says of him:

Mr. Gray was perhaps the most learned man in Europe. He knew every branch of history both natural and civil; had read all the original historians of England, France,

and Italy; and was a great antiquarian.   Criticism, metaphysics, morals, politics, made a principal part of his study.
Voyages and travels of all sorts were his favourite amuse-
ments.

To this should be added that Gray spent many
years in an intensive study of the Greek language
and literature and that he was finally appointed
professor of history in the university.   Now,
Gray once wrote to a friend:

> I rejoice you have met with Froissart, he is the Herodo-
> tus of a barbarous age; had he but had the luck of writing
> in as good a language he might have been immortal.   His
> locomotive disposition (for then there was no other way
> of learning things), his simple curiosity, his religious
> credulity, were much like those of the old Grecian.

Froissart, whose name the poet Gray thus
couples with that of "the old Grecian" was, of
course, not a historian in the scientific meaning
of the word.   He was a traveller and a chroni-
cler.   So was Herodotus.

It is as a traveller and master of story-telling
that I like to think of Herodotus.   I shall not
take the trouble to discuss his merits as a historian, a phase of his genius which seems to me
incidental and to which even so great a critic
as Rawlinson has given disproportionate and unnecessary attention.

It can easily be conceived what an adventure it was to travel even short distances in the Fifth Century before Christ. The saddle, the wheel, the oar, and the sail afforded the only machinery of locomotion for those who were unwilling or unable to walk. The countryside was full of bandits. A description of an earlier age is not wholly inapplicable to the distant parts of Magna Græcia in the time of Herodotus.

It was at that time [says Plutarch, speaking of the days of Theseus], very dangerous to go by land on the road to Athens, no part of it being free from robbers and murderers. That age produced a sort of men, in force of hand, and swiftness of foot, and strength of body, excelling the ordinary rate and wholly incapable of fatigue; making use, however, of these gifts of nature to no good or profitable purpose for mankind, but rejoicing and priding themselves in insolence, and taking the benefit of their superior strength in the exercise of inhumanity and cruelty.

Under what must have been very similar conditions, Herodotus began his travels when he was about nineteen years old and spent twenty years in almost incessantly exploring what was then the known world. He explored the territory from the southern shore of Scythia (now South Russia) on the Black Sea to Egypt, and from Italy to the confines of Persia, an area measuring 1,600 by 1,700 miles. To the modern globetrotter this seems a trifle, but with the conditions of society and of transportation as they existed in the days of Herodotus it was a vast field to cover. When he reached his fortieth year, Herodotus settled in Athens, afterward removing to a Greek colony in southern Italy, where he died when he was about sixty years old. These last twenty years of his life he appears to have devoted to finishing, revising, polishing, and preparing for the public his famous history, which has survived him more than two thousand years and is likely to exist until the tabloid picture-newspapers have destroyed all taste and capacity for English or Classical literature. May the gods postpone this catastrophe for at least two thousand years more!

Nobody knows much, if anything, about the parents of Herodotus or his social position. A writer of the Eleventh Century says that he belonged to an "illustrious" family, but there are no records extant to verify this statement. Suidas, who thus classes Herodotus with the social "four hundred" of Halicarnassus, was a hero-worshipper—a kind of Parson Weems. As the pious biographer of Washington tried to deify his hero, so Suidas may have subconsciously wished to give his favourite author all

the advantages of social breeding and prestige.
But whether Herodotus came from an obscure
or a prominent family, it is quite certain, from
the internal evidence of his writings, that he
received the best education that his day could
afford. Among other things, he learned to play
the flute. According to the Greek legend the
goddess Athena invented the flute, but threw it
away when she discovered that blowing upon
it twisted her face and marred its symmetrical
beauty. The satyr Marsyas picked up Athena's
discarded flute and developed great skill in playing upon it. He was so presumptuous as to
challenge Apollo, the god of the lyre (or the
patron and protector of stringed instruments),
to a contest of musicianship. The umpire decided in favour of Marsyas and suffered, as is
often the lot of umpires, an unhappy fate; for
Apollo used his omnipotence in a very irascible
and godless fashion to endow the umpire with
asses' ears for his poor judgment, and completed
the job by flaying alive the wretched Marsyas.
Thus began the downfall of the flute. Alcibiades completed its debacle. He was a gay young
fellow, handsome, gracious, charming, intellectually brilliant, a crack athlete, and the natural
leader of his generation. But he would not

study music.   In his anecdotal essay on Alcibiades, Plutarch thus tells the story of the young man's musical revolt:

When he began to study, he obeyed all his other masters fairly well, but refused to learn upon the flute as a sordid thing, and not becoming a free citizen; saying that to play on the lute or the harp does not in any way disfigure a man's body or face, but one is hardly to be known by the most intimate friends when playing on the flute.   Besides, one who plays on the harp may speak or sing at the same time; but the use of the flute stops the mouth, intercepts the voice, and prevents all articulation.   "Therefore," said he, "let the Theban youths pipe, who do not know how to speak, but we Athenians, as our ancestors have told us, have Athena for our patroness, and Apollo for our protector, one of whom threw away the flute, and the other stripped the flute-player of his skin."   Thus between raillery and good earnest, Alcibiades kept not only himself but others from learning, as it presently became the talk of the young boys how Alcibiades despised playing on the flute, and ridiculed those who studied it.   In consequence of which it ceased to be reckoned among the liberal accomplishments and became generally neglected.

As Herodotus was more than thirty years older than Alcibiades, he was probably not affected by the anti-flute rebellion.   Whether he played that instrument or not, he certainly had some musical training, for he refers to the piping, or flute playing, and the singing of the Egyptians with the familiarity of one trained in the art. Moreover, no one without musical taste could

have written the story of Arion as Herodotus
tells it:

The Corinthians relate that Arion of Methymna, who as
a player on the harp was second to no man living at that
time, and who was, so far as we know, the first to invent
the dithyrambic measure, to give it its name, and to recite
it at Corinth, was carried to Tænarum on the back of a
dolphin.

He had lived for many years at the court of Periander,
when a longing came upon him to sail across to Italy and
Sicily. Having made rich profits in those parts [Arion
was evidently the Paderewski of his day!], he wanted to
recross the seas to Corinth. He therefore hired a vessel,
the crew of which were Corinthians, thinking that there
was no people in whom he could more safely confide; and
going on board, he set sail from Tarentum. The sailors,
however, when they reached the open sea, formed a plot
to throw him overboard and seize upon his riches. Dis-
covering their design, he fell on his knees, beseeching them
to spare his life, and making them welcome to his money.
But they refused; and required him either to kill himself
outright, if he wished for a grave on the dry land, or without loss of time to leap overboard into the sea. In this
strait Arion begged them, since such was their pleasure, to
allow him to mount upon the quarter-deck, dressed in his
full costume, and there to play and sing, promising that,
as soon as his song was ended, he would destroy himself.
Delighted at the prospect of hearing the very best harper
in the world, they consented, and withdrew from the stern
to the middle of the vessel: while Arion dressed himself in
the full costume of his calling, took his harp, and standing
on the quarter-deck, chanted the Orthian [according to
Rawlinson a lively, spirited air]. His strain ended, he
flung himself, fully attired as he was, headlong into the

sea. The Corinthians then sailed on to Corinth. As for Arion, a dolphin, *they say*, took him upon his back and carried him to Tænarum, where he went ashore and thence walked to Corinth in his musician's dress, and told all that had happened to him. Periander, however, disbelieved the story, and put Arion in ward, to prevent his leaving Corinth, while he watched anxiously for the return of the mariners. On their arrival he summoned them before him and asked if they could give any tidings of Arion. They returned for answer that he was alive and in good health in Italy, and that they had left him at Tarentum, where he was doing well. Thereupon Arion appeared before them, just as he was when he jumped from the vessel: and the men, astonished and detected in falsehood, could no longer deny their guilt.

Such is the account which the Corinthians and Lesbians give; and there is to this day at Tænarum an offering of Arion's at the shrine, which is a small figure in bronze, representing a man seated upon a dolphin.

Whatever may have been the attitude of Herodotus toward music, he must have been faithful in his gymnastic and classical studies. No man could have spent twenty years as he did in arduous and often dangerous travel without a sound and well-developed body and muscles. His reference to the accepted writers of the educated world of his day are frequent. With the writings of Homer he shows the most complete and critical familiarity. In one instance he refers to a writing ascribed to Homer with the comment, "If that be really a work of his."

The charm of Herodotus for the layman lies not in his value as a historian but in his genius as an anecdotist. The story of Arion already quoted well illustrates his delightful and, in some respects, incomparable talent for story-telling. Of a similar character are the tales of Candaules, who lost his life and his kingdom because, out of vain pride, he contrived to exhibit his wife's undraped physical charms to an intimate friend who was a member of his body-guard; the narrative of the capture of Crœsus by Cyrus; the report of the very modern denunciation of war by Crœsus as a procedure "in which, instead of sons burying their fathers, fathers bury their sons"; and the amusing anecdote of Alcmæon, which, as it shows that Herodotus possessed a blessed sense of humour, deserves to be quoted in full:

Crœsus, informed of Alcmæon's kindnesses . . . sent for him to Sardis, and when he arrived, made him a present of as much gold as he should be able to carry at one time about his person. Finding that this was the gift assigned to him, Alcmæon took his measures, and prepared himself to receive it in the following way. He clothed himself in a loose tunic, which he made to bag greatly at the waist, and placing upon his feet the widest buskins that he could anywhere find, followed his guides into the treasure house. Here he fell to upon a heap of gold-dust, and in the first place packed as much as he could inside his buskins, between them and his legs; after which he filled the breast of his tunic quite full of gold, and then sprinkling some among his hair, and taking some likewise in his mouth, he came forth from the treasure house, scarcely able to drag his legs along, like anything rather than a man, with his mouth crammed full, and his bulk increased in every way. On seeing him, Crœsus burst into a laugh, and not only let him have all that he had taken, but gave him presents besides of fully equal worth. Thus this house [the Alcmæonidæ] became one of great wealth; and Alcmæon was able to keep horses for the chariot race, and won the prize at Olympia.

Thus were created the Astors and the Vanderbilts, the Russells and the Rothschilds of ancient times, and thus originated the prize-winning prototypes of our great polo players, yachtsmen, and Derby winners!

Herodotus was a modern in being familiar with great works of engineering and construction. If he could come back to earth, he would doubtless be amazed by our steamships and electric elevators, but he would not stand agape at the excavations of the Panama Canal or at the height of the towering skyscrapers of New York; for he describes the wonders of Babylon quite calmly and without any special note of astonishment, merely recording in a matter-of-fact manner its size, magnificence, and the dimensions of its famous wall. If his figures were correct, the Great Wall of Babylon would have enclosed an area several times that of London, would have been more than three hundred feet in height, and would have contained, according to Rawlinson's estimate, more than two hundred million yards of solid masonry. The researches of archæologists reduce these figures somewhat, but that Herodotus was perfectly honest in stating them and was not influenced by a spirit either of credulity or of conscious exaggeration may be assumed from evidence which his own writing furnishes. In describing the Great Wall he says:

On the topmost tower there is a spacious temple, and inside the temple stands a couch of unusual size, richly adorned, with a golden table by its side. . . . The Chaldeans . . . declare—*but I for my part do not credit it*—that the god comes down in person into this chamber, and sleeps upon the couch.

The words which I have italicized dispose of the accusation that Herodotus was an extremely credulous person. Similar caveats scattered through all his history indicate that he was cautious both as an investigator and recorder. During his visit to Egypt, Herodotus saw the great pyramid of Cheops just outside of Cairo. This he also describes in a calm fashion. Its dimensions as he gives them are reasonably accurate. He says that the pyramid is eight hundred feet square on its base. It is really seven hundred and thirty-two feet square on its base—not a very serious discrepancy. A more serious difference in figures is involved in his statement that the height of the pyramid is eight hundred feet. The truth is that its original apex was about four hundred and eighty feet above the base. Since Herodotus says that he measured the pyramid himself, his critics have hailed his apparent error about its height as a striking evidence of his unreliability. But Rawlinson points out that Herodotus had no means of measuring the vertical height by triangulation and so measured the length of the slope from the base to the apex by hand, actually a distance of over seven hundred feet. This he may well have regarded as the height of the colossal monument. His carefulness of observation is shown in some other statistics of the pyramid which he records. He says that some hieroglyphics on its surface (these surface stones having disappeared since his day) named "the quantity of radishes, onions, and garlic consumed by the labourers who constructed it; and I perfectly well remember that the interpreter who read the writing to me said that the money expended in this way was 16,000 talents of silver"—a sum equivalent to about two millions of dollars in our money. Herodotus adds quite pertinently, "If this then is a true record, what a vast sum must have been spent" on the essential cost of tools, stone quarrying, and the maintenance for thirty or forty years of a hundred thousand slave labourers. The gigantic achievement of the builder of the great pyramids did not blind Herodotus to his despotic and despicable character, for the Father of History repeats this story, which was told him by one of the interpreters:

The wickedness of Cheops reached to such a pitch that when he had spent all his treasures and wanted more he sent his daughter to the brothels with orders to procure him a certain sum—how much I cannot say, for I was not told; she procured it, however, and at the same time, bent on leaving a monument which should perpetuate her own memory, she required each man who visited her to make her a present of a stone toward the works which she contemplated. With these stones she built the pyramid which stands midmost of the three that are in front of the great pyramid, measuring along each side a hundred and fifty feet.

This charming tale of parental care, like the somewhat similar but more elaborate story of Rhampsinitus and his daughter, were very likely repeated by Herodotus as merely interesting gossip and not because of their historical value.

For it must not be supposed that Herodotus

as a historian made no attempt to discriminate between what he saw with his own eyes, or what he believed to be actual events, and what he regarded as legendary tales or folklore. At the very beginning of his book, in relating the migrations of the ancient Barbarians and their raids upon the Greeks, he says that there are two accounts of the matter, adding:

which of the two accounts is true I shall not trouble to decide; I shall proceed at once to point out the person who first within my own knowledge commenced aggressions on the Greeks, after which I shall go forward with my history, describing equally the lesser and the greater cities.

And later, when he comes to relate the experiences and impressions of his memorable tour through Egypt, he more than once cautions the reader not to be too credulous. For example, he describes his visit to an old battlefield where he saw on one side a pile of Persian skulls and on the other a pile of Egyptian skulls.

If you strike the Persian skulls [he says], even with a pebble, they are so weak that you break a hole in them; but the Egyptian skulls are so strong, that you may smite them with a stone and you will scarcely break them in. They gave me the following reason for this difference, which seemed to me likely enough. The Egyptians, they said, from early childhood have the head shaved, and so by the action of the sun the skull becomes thick and hard.

. . . The Persians, on the other hand, have feeble skulls, because they keep themselves shaded from their youth up, wearing turbans upon their heads. What I have here mentioned I saw with my own eyes.

And then to make assurance doubly sure, he covers the entire Egyptian phase of his reminiscences with this general *caveat:*

Such as think the tales told by the Egyptians credible are free to accept them for history: for my own part, I propose to myself throughout my whole work faithfully to record the traditions of the several nations.

In his political philosophy Herodotus was singularly moderate and dispassionate. He frequently alludes to the desirability of political liberty, and in one passage he says specifically of the progress, under a democratic form of government, of the Athenians whom he greatly admired:

It is plain enough, not from this instance only, but from many everywhere, that freedom is an excellent thing; since even the Athenians, who, while they continued under the rule of tyrants, were not a whit more valiant than any of their neighbours, no sooner shook off the yoke than they became decidedly the first of all.

But with some doubt, apparently, of the supreme wisdom of democracies, a doubt which has been shared in modern times by such patriots as Alexander Hamilton and Lord Bryce, he quotes in full, and if not with approval at least without protest, the speech of Megabyzus, the Persian chief. While Cambyses, the son of Cyrus the Great, was invading Egypt about forty years before Herodotus, two Magian priests or sooth-sayers seized his throne. Darius, Otanes, and Megabyzus, together with three other conspira-tors, overthrew the Magian usurpers. Where-upon a debate ensued as to what form of gov-ernment should be established in their place. Otanes the radical was for a popular democracy, following the practice of the Greeks; Darius the conservative was for a monarchy, and finally won his point; Megabyzus, the liberal or moder-ate, was for an oligarchy. The whole debate is entertaining and well worth reading, but I will quote only the argument of Megabyzus, for I am inclined to think that it reflects the inmost philosophy of Herodotus:

In all that Otanes has said to persuade you to put down monarchy, I fully concur; but his recommendation that we should call the people to power seems to me not the best advice. For there is nothing so void of understand-ing, nothing so full of wantonness, as the unwieldy rabble. It were folly not to be borne for men, while seeking to es-cape the wantonness of a tyrant, to give themselves up to the wantonness of a rude, unbridled mob. The tyrant,

in all his doings, at least knows what he is about, but a
mob is altogether devoid of knowledge; for how should
there be any knowledge in a rabble, untaught and with no
natural sense of what is right and fit? It rushes wildly
into state affairs with all the fury of a stream swollen in
the winter, and confusing everything. Let the enemies
of the Persians be ruled by democracies; but let us choose
out from the citizens a certain number of the worthiest,
and put the government into their hands. For thus both
we ourselves shall be among the governors [this was perhaps a sop to Darius, the unlimited monarchist], and
power being entrusted to the best men, it is likely that the
best councils will prevail in the state.

May it not be inferred that Herodotus was a
believer in a representative government rather
than town-meeting democracy. And if he had
lived in our era, would he not have been a
Federalist of the school of John Marshall rather
than a popularist of the school of Thomas Jefferson?

From the point of view of political history,
the great book of Herodotus is an account of the
struggle between the Greeks, chiefly represented
by the Athenians, and the Barbarians, chiefly
represented by the Persians. It begins somewhat abruptly by introducing the Persians and
ends with equal abruptness by bidding them farewell. Some critics have felt that Herodotus
was cut off by death before his twenty years'
labour of polishing and revising had been com-

pleted, and that he was thus prevented from finishing his work by adding the epilogue which he must have had in mind. Others think that the apparently chopped-off conclusion of Herodotus's book is really a stroke of consummate art. Whatever may be the decision in this matter the concluding passage of the Herodotean history is an example of the dramatic power of simplicity. This passage relates how Cyrus the Great was overpersuaded by his Persian subjects to begin his invasion of Greece; how the Greeks finally defeated a succeeding generation of Persians and crucified Artayctes, "one of their wicked and cruel satraps"; and how the Persians then departed acknowledging their foolishness.

It was the grandfather of this Artayctes, one Artembares by name, who first suggested to the Persians a proposal which they readily embraced, and thus urged upon Cyrus: —"Since Jove has given the rule to the Persians, and to thee chiefly, O Cyrus! come now, let us quit this land wherein we dwell—for it is a scant land and rugged—and let us choose ourselves some other better country. Many such lie around us, some nearer, some further off: if we take one of these, men will admire us far more than they do now. Who that had the power would not so act? And when shall we have a fairer time than now, when we are the lords of so many nations, and rule all Asia?" Then Cyrus, who did not greatly esteem the counsel, told them,—"they might do so if they liked—but not to expect in that case to continue rulers, but to prepare for being ruled by others

—soft countries give birth to soft men—there was no region which produced very delightful fruits, and at the same time men of a warlike spirit." So the Persians departed with altered minds, confessing that Cyrus was wiser than they; and choose rather to dwell in a churlish land, and exercise lordship, than to cultivate plains, and be the slave of others.

In the essay with which Rawlinson introduces his translation of Herodotus, he makes clear the outstanding qualities of the old Grecian's immortal book—its epic unity, its entertaining episodes, its human characterizations, and its ever-refreshing variety. Herodotus was historian, biographer, naturalist, mythologist, moralist, antiquarian, and traveller all in one. He has sometimes been called the first great prose writer. To this definition should be added a limiting phrase. Herodotus may only safely be named the first great prose writer *of the Western world;* for Confucius preceded Herodotus by a full generation, was the founder of Chinese literature, and a master of prose writing. But Confucius was not a traveller or explorer. He was a meditator, and his inspiration was derived from his inner consciousness.

It is no small thing to strike out an original prose style or to write a historical chronicle that lasts for centuries. But it is not as a stylist or historian that I have chosen Herodotus to lead my little company of twelve. It is as an indefatigable traveller and as a shrewd, wise, witty, and sympathetic observer of the virtues and frailties of mankind that he is entitled to be called the first of the Modernists.

ST. FRANCIS OF ASSISI

THE WORLDLING

Two: St. Francis of Assisi

THE WORLDLING

BORN 1182—DIED 1226

IN OCTOBER of last year, the year of our
Lord 1926, thousands of devout men and
women remembered and observed the seven
hundredth anniversary of the death of one of the
gentlest saints and most romantic figures of
Christendom, St. Francis of Assisi. Someone
will quite naturally ask why this mediæval saint,
who abjured riches and espoused poverty, should
be included in a group of modernists, since fondness for prosperity and dislike of asceticism are
two marked characteristics of modern life. The
answer is that, although a saint, Francis was
no ascetic. He was neither denunciatory like
Savonarola nor lugubrious like Bunyan. He was
full of *joie de vivre*, the joy of being alive. He
thanked God for the beauties of nature and the
unalloyed pleasures of companionship. He was
preëminently a lover of man and of nature, that
is to say, a lover of the world as we see it. "Religious formalism," says his distinguished Protes-

tant biographer, Paul Sabatier, "in whatever form of worship, always takes on a forced and morose manner. Pharisees of every age disfigure their faces that no one may be unaware of their godliness. Francis not merely could not endure these grimaces of false piety, he actually counted mirth and joy in the number of religious duties."

It is true that Francis enjoined upon the active members of his order the abandonment of all material possessions and urged them to live by manual labour or, when necessary, upon charity, but this was in order that they might be freed from slavery to things and at complete liberty to carry on their preaching mission. He did not denounce riches *per se*. He was not a Socialist but a Salvationist. His attitude toward wealth was like that of his mother church toward celibacy. Rome does not command every man to be a celibate; on the contrary, she commends and encourages marriage. She only insists that her special ministers shall be relieved of the responsibilities of family life in order that they may carry on single-heartedly the particular work to which they are ordained.

Francis [says one of his sympathetic biographers] did not war against rich men. He was all the more a social solvent that he made no cut and dried scheme of social

reform. . . . Riches might be used well. He did not
set up to be the judge of their possessors, and especially
enjoined his brothers not to do so. But there was a royal
road to freedom of the spirit, and that was to have none of
them. . . . To make the whole world Franciscan
was not in Francis's mind. He was but concerned to train
his own little army for the service of the world.

Romantic and gentle as he was, it was neither
the gentleness nor the romance of St. Francis
that first drew me to him; it was his love of
human companionship. This joyous, human
quality of St. Francis, and of his early followers,
is a thing quite distinct from the spiritual joy
and serenity which saints of all ages have professed. St. Francis felt very profoundly his
kinship with God, but equally profoundly his
kinship with man. The philologists throw quite
as much light on St. Francis as the theologians.
The word humanist has its origin, they tell us,
in the Latin words *homo*, man, and *humus*, the
earth. The humanist is "one versed in human
affairs and relations"; he is, therefore, deeply
interested in the earthly, bodily life of man.
The Puritans were not humanists—they were
spiritualists. Like all ascetics, they were afraid
of the body. St. Anthony was their model,
not St. Francis. To St. Francis the world was
beautiful and the human race was blessed by
being placed in it. I do not find in his sermons

any lugubrious talk about the fall of man or
about his being chained to the body of this
death.   Life seemed to him full of happy associations.

This spirit of human contentment appears
definitely in the very creed which St. Francis
wrote, and it peeps out frequently in the legends
or stories which were woven about his name by
his devoted followers, and which are known as
the *Fioretti*, or "Little Flowers."   He had an
appreciation of the droll and the comic.   On one
occasion, in an exhortation to his disciples, he
went so far as to point his moral with an excellent pun.   Sabatier says that "in the history of
the early Franciscan Mission there are bursts
of laughter which ring out high and clear."

It was Paul Sabatier's biography which, about
thirty years ago, first attracted my attention to
St. Francis and the quality of his humour.   From
that biography I learned that one of the precepts
of the Rule of the Franciscan Order, a Rule which
is believed to come from the hand of the Saint
himself, inculcates a sense of humour.   This
precept reads, in the colloquial Latin which St.
Francis wrote and spoke, as follows:

Caveant fratres quod non ostendant se tristes extrinsi-
cus, nubilosos et hypocritas; sed ostendant se gaudentes in
Domine, hilares et convenienter gratiosos.

The precept may be fairly put into English in these words:

Let the brothers take care not to appear long-faced, gloomy, or overpious; but let them be joyous about their faith in God, laughing and agreeable companions.

I once translated *convenienter gratiosos* by the term "good mixers." But I found this colloquialism grated slightly on the ears of a good friend of mine, a devout Catholic, who felt that it was a little inappropriate to apply so modern a phrase to so sanctified a spirit as St. Francis. But why not? The great Master of St. Francis was accused by the conventionalists of his day of being a mixer with publicans and sinners; and a conservative and entirely respectable British journal, the *Quarterly Review*, recently said that the *gratiosus* side of Jesus has been too much neglected. In reviewing Bruce Barton's *The Man Nobody Knows*, which may almost be called a colloquial life of Jesus, the *Quarterly* remarks that the book "brings out admirably that side of the personality of Christ which superstition has denied to him—his joy of life, his laughter, qualities which he must have possessed if he were to win (as he did win) the hearts of children and of the everyday multitude."

This power of attraction St. Francis also possessed—and quite naturally. His father was a rich merchant and his mother a lady of the gentry. Intended to be a wealthy business man and supplied by his father with plenty of money and leisure, he was a gay, lively, and popular young man about town. He even went to the wars in search of mundane glory. But after a sudden conversion, which some people like to think not less miraculous than St. Paul's, he abandoned wealth and war and became the apostle of poverty and peace. But he never was, like some of the saints on the calendar, an eremite; to the end of his comparatively short, but superlatively influential, career he maintained his love of life, of joy, and of the beauties of nature. Nor, apparently, did he entirely lose the power of employing the language of the trenches and the camps, for an ardent disciple and companion, Thomas of Celano, tells us that on one occasion he vented his indignation on a friar who showed a too great fondness for the society of ladies, in words scarcely suitable to be literally repeated in the biography of a saint. His instinctive gaiety sometimes cropped out in an unexpected way. The same contemporary biographer who describes his vigorous denunciation of the amorous friar says that more than

once he saw St. Francis take a stick and drawing
it across his arm like a fiddle bow on a fiddle,
sing psalms of praises to the Lord in French; and
French was preëminently the joyous language of
his time. Perhaps these hymns were his own
composition. There is one still in existence,
which is at least ascribed to him, the famous
"Hymn to the Sun." It was doubtless suggested to him by the 148th Psalm. In it he
calls upon all creatures to praise the Lord,
especially Brother Sun, radiant and splendid;
and Sister Moon, luminous and lovely in the
sky; and Brother Wind, the master of cloud and
fair weather; and Sister Water, precious and
pure; and Brother Fire, luminous, mighty, and
strong; and Mother Earth, who gives us fruits
and flowers of many colours. The man who
wrote this surely loved the world and its beauties.

He loved, too, in a way, if the *Fioretti* may be
believed, the very foolishness of men. Among
his favourites was a Friar Juniper, who was all
the time doing the most senseless things by way
of expressing his faith and devotion, and all the
time exciting equally the vexation, the amusement, and the compassion of St. Francis. From
the Juniper stories related in the *Fioretti* I
select one which is especially delightful, so it
seems to me, for its literary charm and the

pleasant light it throws on the humanism of the
Assisian Saint.   It is here offered in the translation of Thomas Okey of Cambridge University:

Friar Juniper was one of the most chosen disciples and
first companions of St. Francis.   He was a man of deep
humility and of great zeal and charity; and of him St.
Francis said, speaking on a time with those holy companions of his, "He were a good friar that had so overcome
himself and the world as Friar Juniper hath."   One day,
as he was visiting a sick friar at St. Mary of the Angels, all
aflame with charity, he asked with great compassion,
"Can I serve thee in aught?"   The sick man answers,
"Much comfort and great solace would it be to me if I
might have a pig's foot."   And Friar Juniper said, "Trust
to me, for I will get one forthwith."   And off he goes and
snatches up a knife (I believe 'twas a kitchen knife) and
goes in fervour of spirit about the wood, where certain
pigs were feeding, and falling on one of them, cuts off a
foot and runs away with it, leaving the pig maimed; he
returns, washes and dresses and cooks this foot, and having
well dished it up, carries the said foot to the sick man with
much charity.   And the sick friar ate thereof greedily,
to the great consolation and joy of Friar Juniper, who told
the story of the assaults he had made on the pig with great
glee, to rejoice the heart of the sick man.   Meanwhile the
swineherd, that saw this friar cut the foot off, told over
the whole story with much bitterness to his master.   And
he, being informed of this deed, comes to the friary and
calls the friars hypocrites, thieves, false knaves, and wicked
rogues, exclaiming, "Wherefore have ye cut off my pig's
foot?"   Hearing the great uproar he made, St. Francis
and all the friars hurried along, and St. Francis made excuse for his friars, saying, with all humility, that they knew
naught of the deed; and to pacify the man, promised to

make amends for every wrong done him.   But for all this he was not to be appeased, but departed from the friary in great wrath, uttering many insults and threats, repeating over and over again how that they had wickedly cut off his pig's foot, and accepting neither excuses nor promises, he hastened away greatly scandalized.   But St. Francis, full of prudence, bethought him the while the other friars stood all stupefied, and said in his heart, "Can Friar Juniper have done this thing out of indiscreet zeal?"   So he bade them call Friar Juniper secretly to him, and asked him, saying, "Hast thou cut off that pig's foot in the wood?"   To whom Friar Juniper answered, right gleefully and not as one having committed a fault, but as one that believed he had done a deed of great charity, and spake thus, "My sweet father, true it is I have cut off a foot from that said pig; and the cause thereof, my father, hear, if thou wilt, compassionately.   I went out of charity to visit a certain friar that was sick"; and then he related the whole story in order, and added, "I tell thee this much, that considering the consolation this friar of ours felt, and the comfort he took from the said foot, had I cut off the feet of a hundred pigs as I did this one, I believe of a surety God would have looked on it as a good deed."   Whereupon St. Francis, with righteous zeal, and with great bitterness, said, "O Friar Juniper, wherefore hast thou wrought this great scandal?   Not without cause doth that man grieve, and thus rail against us; and perchance even now, as I speak, he is going about the city defaming us of evil, and good cause hath he.   Wherefore I command thee, by holy obedience, run after him until thou overtake him, and cast thyself on the ground prostrate before him and confess thy fault, and promise to make him such full amends as that he shall have no cause to complain of us: for of a surety this has been too monstrous an offence." Friar Juniper marvelled much at the aforesaid words, and

was filled with amaze, being astonished that there should
be any disturbance over such an act of charity; for these
temporal things seemed to him naught, save in so far as
they were charitably shared with one's neighbour.   And
Friar Juniper answered, "Fear not, father mine, for anon
will I repay him and make him content.   And wherefore
should he be so troubled, seeing that this pig, whose foot
I have cut off, was God's rather than his own, and a very
charitable use hath been made thereof?"   And so he sets
forth at a run, and cometh up with this man that was
raging beyond all measure and past all patience; and he
told him how, and for what cause, he had cut off the said
pig's foot, and withal in such great fervour and exultation
and joy, even as one that had done him a great service for
which he ought to be well rewarded.   But the man, boiling
with anger, and overcome with fury, heaped many insults
on Friar Juniper, calling him a mad fellow and a fool, a
big thief, and the worst of scoundrels.   But Friar Juniper
cared naught for these abusive words, and marvelled
within himself, for he rejoiced in being reviled, and
believed that he had not heard aright; for it seemed to him
matter for rejoicing, and not for spite: and he told the
story anew, and fell on the man's neck and embraced him
and kissed him, and told him how that this thing had been
done for charity's sake alone, inviting him and entreating
him to give likewise what was left of the pig; and all with
such charity and simplicity and humility that the man,
being come to himself, fell on the ground before him, not
without many tears; and asking pardon for the wrong he
had said and done to these friars, he goes and takes this
pig and kills it, and having cooked it he carries it, with
much devotion and many tears, to St. Mary of the Angels,
and gives it to these holy friars to eat, out of compassion
for the said wrong he had done them.   And St. Francis,
considering the simplicity and the patience under adversity

of this said holy friar, said to his companions and to the others that stood by, "Would to God, my brethren, that I had a whole forest of such junipers!"

A modern characteristic of St. Francis, which, however, is as ancient as the prophet Micah, was that he laid little stress on metaphysical theology and great emphasis on right human relationships. He had not a trace of scepticism in his temperament and doubtless accepted without question the dogmas of his church. Yet it is singular how little of theological reasoning there is in any of his writings or in the writings of his contemporaries about him. The story of Friar Juniper is typical of the genuine simplicity of this altogether human saint. The Life of St. Francis written by one of his followers, St. Bonaventura, not many years after the death of the Founder, is full of this engaging naïveté:

If [says Bonaventura] Francis beheld any man wandering about in idleness, and fain to feed on the toil of others, he thought he ought to be called "Brother Fly" for that, doing no good himself, and spoiling the good done by others, he made himself a hateful pest unto all.

And again, another passage:

The vice of slander, hateful unto the fount of goodness and grace, Francis would shrink from as from a serpent's tooth, declaring it to be a most hateful plague, and an abomination unto the most holy God, forasmuch as the slanderer feedeth on the blood of those souls that he hath slain by the sword of his tongue. Hearing once a certain Brother blacken the repute of another, he turned unto his Vicar, and said, "Rise, rise, make careful enquiry, and, if thou findest the accused Brother to be guiltless, with stern discipline make the accuser to be marked of all." At times, indeed, he would sentence him who had despoiled his Brother of the praise of his good repute to be himself despoiled of his habit, and deemed that he ought not to be able to lift his eyes unto God unless first he had exerted himself to restore, as best he might, that which he had taken away. "The sin of slanderers," he would say, "is more heinous than that of robbers, inasmuch as the law of Christ—that is fulfilled in the observance of godliness— bindeth us to desire more the salvation of the soul than of the body."

This analysis of the vice of slander may have been in the mind of the author of Othello when he wrote:

Who steals my purse steals trash; 'tis something, nothing;
'Twas mine, 'tis his and has been slave to thousands.
But he that filches from me my good name
Robs me of that which not enriches him,
And makes me poor indeed.

Another modern quality of St. Francis was his love of animals. In the Hebraic and mediæval Christian theology the beasts of the field were not merely dumb animals, they were damned animals. They had no souls. Their inheritance from the tragedy of the Garden of Eden was a

satanic character. In the Old Testament the
dog is a symbol of the utmost contempt. In
Deuteronomy it is recorded:

Thou shalt not bring the hire of a whore, or the price of a
dog into the house of the Lord thy God for any vow; for
even both these are abominations unto the Lord thy God.

And when Elisha prophesied that Ben-hadad,
the Syrian king, would dash the Israelitish children on the stones and "rip up their women with
child," the King's ambassador in great indignation exclaimed, "What! is thy servant a dog
that he should do this great thing?" In the
Middle Ages one might cudgel his ass with as little
compunction as he flailed his grain. But with
Francis it was always Brother Ass and Brother
Wolf, Sister Locust and Sister Bird. He had in
the quaint language of Bonaventura, "such
wondrous sweetness and might as that it con-
quered wild beasts, tamed woodland creatures
and taught tame ones, and inclined the nature of
brutes, that had revolted from fallen man, to
obey him."

His mighty sweetness is attested, too, by one
of the pleasantest stories about him—that of
his sermon to the birds. On one of his preaching missions he stopped by the wayside and said
to his companions, "Tarry here for me by the

way, and I will go and preach to my little sisters, the birds." Whereupon he bade the birds be grateful to their Creator for the feathers with which they were clothed, for the wings with which they could fly, and for the pure air into which they could soar. And the birds, it is related, acknowledged the lesson by stretching their necks, spreading their wings, opening their beaks, and looking intently on him. By the devout this is regarded as one of the miraculous signs of the saintship of St. Francis. It is rather, I think, a sign of his humanistic wisdom. By choosing the birds as a congregation and professing to preach to them on the duty of gratitude he was really taking the surest and most captivating route to the ears and hearts of his human hearers.

It is well for St. Francis that he had this understanding of human frailty and human nobility, for without it he must have been unutterably sad. No man in history has been actuated by a more genuine and passionate love of peace, simplicity, and brotherly kindness. He lived to see the brotherhood which he founded become a highly complex organization, possessing large properties and torn with sectarianism. Even his last illness was tainted by the love of money on the part of some of his followers—a

love which he tried so hard to eradicate during
his devoted life.

In March, 1226 [says Professor Thomas Okey], he was
under a famous physician at Siena. Admonished by a
severe hemorrhage, he dictated his spiritual Testament to
Benedict of Prato—a last touching appeal for the pure,
strict, and single-minded observance of his Rule. After
a short rest at Cortona, where dropsy set in, Friar Elias had
the death-stricken saint carried to Assisi, and at Bagnora
the sorrowful procession was met by an armed force sent
by the authorities at Assisi, who were fearful lest the men
of the rival city of Perugia might snatch the body and
thus deprive them of its lucrative possession.

In spite of this touch of lucre, Assisi has been
for seven hundred years, and will continue to be
for seven hundred years to come, the mecca for
those who are inspired by truth, simplicity,
brotherly kindness, self-sacrifice, and devotion
to an ideal when they see these divine qualities
displayed in a fellow human being. That I
should have called St. Francis "The Worldling"
may seem to some a shocking perversion of
terms. I have done so deliberately. In spirit
a saint, on his human side he loved the world,
its beauty, its companionship of men and women.
The great lesson he taught, as I think Jesus
taught it, was how men may live together in this
world without envy, greed, or cruelty—whatever
may be the life of the world to come.

ERASMUS

THE EMANCIPATOR

THE EMANCIPATOR
BORN 1466 OR 7—DIED 1536

COURAGE, mon ami, le diable est mort!
Cheer up, my boy, the devil is dead.

This slogan of incorrigible optimism Charles Reade puts in the mouth of the delightful Burgundian soldier, Denis, in that most picturesque of all English historical novels, *The Cloister and the Hearth.* It might be ascribed to Erasmus as his motto. For Erasmus spent his life in struggling with the devils of ignorance, superstition, and intolerance and in freeing the mind from slavery to them. In this struggle he employed ripe scholarship, vivid description, and cutting ridicule and may fairly be called the founder of the modern school of epistolary and satirical literature. Both in spirit and in manner he was one of the first of the Modernists, and it is a pity that he cannot return to earth to-day to wield his trenchant pen, as he did during his lifetime, against those who would throttle a simple, reasonable, and lovable Christianity by enveloping it in a mass of man-made philosophies and theologies.

The general reader, to whom Latin is anathema and the textual scholarship of meticulous Germans a bore and a stumbling block, and yet who wishes to understand why Erasmus is one of the brightest stars in the endless literary firmament, cannot make a better beginning than by reading *The Cloister and the Hearth*. It is imagined to be the love story of Gerard and Margaret, the father and mother of Erasmus, and gives a more vivid picture of the social, moral, ecclesiastical, and political customs of the time of Erasmus than can be found in more serious and accurate histories and biographies. After getting from this story an impression of the state of Europe when Erasmus was born, the reader may intelligently turn to the *Life and Letters of Erasmus*, by the English historian, Froude; to *Erasmus, a Study of His Life, Ideals and Place in History*, by the American historian, Dr. Preserved Smith of Cornell University; and to *The Epistles of Erasmus*, edited by F. M. Nichols. To these three works I am chiefly indebted for the facts of this brief essay.

Erasmus was born in Holland—by some supposed to be an illegitimate child—about the middle of the Fifteenth Century. The exact year of his birth is uncertain because of the variation of his own statements. At that time the terrible despotism of the Roman Catholic theocracy was at its height in Europe. The life of no man who pretended to think for himself was worth a farthing. It was a time not merely of intellectual repression but of physical suffering and torture. The story of the cruelties practised by Philip II of Spain, who came upon the scene about the time Erasmus left it, is enough to make one's blood boil. No one can read Motley's *Rise of the Dutch Republic* without almost hoping that there might be a hell of eternal torment for inquisitors who, in the name of religion, maimed and tortured men's bodies in the most incredible fashion. Even as late as 1757, the Archbishop Elector of Cologne issued a tariff which—I quote from Dr. Andrew D. White's *Seven Great Statesmen*—"may be seen in the library of Cornell University; on four printed folio pages, it enumerates in fifty-five paragraphs, every sort of hideous cruelty which an executioner could commit upon a prisoner, with the sum allowed him for each, and for the instruments therein required."

According to this tariff, the executioner was paid five thalers for tearing asunder with four horses, four thalers for burning alive, four thalers for breaking a man alive on the wheel, three thalers and a fraction for cutting off a hand or sundry fingers and for beheading, a fraction of a thaler for each tearing with red-hot pincers of the flesh of a criminal before his execution, etc., etc. Such tortures were imposed chiefly, not for criminal deeds, but for heretical opinions in theology. The Protestants, when they got on top, were often not much better than the Catholics. It was this kind of thing that led the framers of our Constitution in 1789 to prohibit the infliction of cruel and unusual punishments.

Erasmus must have been familiar with the physical cruelties of theological despotism. But I do not find in such letters of his as I have read any outstanding protest against physical tortures. He was always a Catholic conformist, never renounced his priesthood, and avoided an open break with the authorities. It was this moderation which turned his contemporary Luther into an angry critic of his course. In times of political or theological convulsion there are always two types of leaders: the fighters or organizers and the critics or stimulators. Luther was of the first type, Erasmus of the second. Unlike Luther, Erasmus was not interested in establishing a new creed. He was an opponent

literary and classical studies. There he met
the enlightened Englishman, Lord Mountjoy,
inter nobiles doctissimus, as Erasmus called him.
Through Mountjoy's good offices Erasmus ulti-
mately visited England and became acquainted
with Prince Henry, afterward Henry VIII, with
whom he was later sometimes associated on
terms of almost intimate friendship. When
Henry VIII got into trouble with Rome, Erasmus was having his own difficulties with that
almost irresistible power. The two came together again at Calais in the summer of 1520 for
a conference about the perplexities which they
shared in common. A contemporary, who was a
loyal Catholic and hated Erasmus because he
did not openly denounce Luther, thus describes
the interview[1]:

I will tell you something of Erasmus. He is a scoundrel.
Hear what he did. He was summoned by the King of
England to take counsel while he was here. The King
slapped him on the back and said: "Why don't you defend
that good man Luther?" Erasmus answered, "Because I
am not enough of a theologian; since Louvain has given
me the robe of a grammarian I meddle with no such business." After many words the King said, "You are a good
fellow, Erasmus," and sent him away with fifty ducats.

A little schoolgirl, in an examination in English
history, once said that Henry VIII was the most

[1] Preserved Smith's *Life of Erasmus.*

interesting king of England. When asked the reason for this surprising statement, she replied that it was because Henry VIII had more wives than children—a sound answer both for the historian and the anthropologist. There is a better reason why Henry VIII should appeal to the lover of intellectual freedom. He was the patron and protector of Erasmus when that priest and scholar was struggling for a revival of untrammelled learning and unadulterated piety. Erasmus was grateful for this protection and expressed his appreciation in a letter to the King which Froude quotes with the somewhat extravagant comment, "I seriously believe that this will be the final verdict of English history on Henry VIII":

To you is due the highest praise. No prince is better prepared for war, and none more wishes to avoid it, knowing, as you do, how deadly a scourge is war to the mass of mankind, while you have so well used your respite that you have cleared the roads of robbers— so long the scourge and reproach of England; you have suppressed vagabonds; you have strengthened your laws, repealed the bad ones, and supplied defects. You have encouraged learning. You have improved discipline among the monks and clergy. You have recognized that a pure and noble race of men is a finer ornament to your realm than warlike trophies or splendid edifices. You make yourself the pattern of what you prescribe for others. The king's command goes far, but the king's example goes further. Who better keeps the law than you keep it? Who seeks less unworthy objects? Who is truer to his word? Who is juster and fairer in all that he does? In what household, in what college or university will you find more wisdom and integrity than in the Court of England? The poet's golden age, if such age ever was, comes back under your Highness. What friend of England does not now congratulate her? What enemy does not envy her good fortune? By their monarchs' character realms are ennobled or depraved. Future ages will tell how England throve, how virtue flourished in the reign of Henry VIII, how the nation was born again, how piety revived, how learning grew to a height which Italy may envy, and how the prince who reigned over it was a rule and pattern for all time to come. Once I avoided kings and courts. Now I would gladly migrate to England if my infirmities allowed. I am but a graft upon her—not a native; yet, when I remember the years which I spent there, the friends I found there, the fortune, small though it be, which I owe her, I rejoice in England's felicity as if she were my natural mother. . . . For yourself, the intelligence of your country will preserve the memory of your virtues, and scholars will tell how a king once reigned there who in his own person revived the virtue of the ancient heroes.

Some exceptions may be taken to the personal encomiums of this letter; Huxley, for instance, in a sarcastic passage of one of his essays, brackets Henry VIII with Judas Iscariot, Robespierre, and Cataline. Nevertheless, this letter of Erasmus is, at least, a fine example of what tact and literary skill may do to impart commendable moral instruction under the form of panegyric.

Although born on the very edge of Germany, Teutonic civilization did not have for Erasmus the charms of life in England. Here is a little picture of German customs and manners paraphrased by Froude from one of the numerous and lively letters which Erasmus wrote to a German friend and fellow scholar, Beatus Rhenanus by name:

Listen to the tragedy of my adventures. I left Bâle relaxed and worn out as one out of favour with the Gods. The river part of my journey was well enough, save for the heat of the sun. We dined at Breisach. Dinner abominable. Foul smells and flies in swarms. We were kept waiting half an hour while the precious banquet was preparing. There was nothing that I could eat, every dish filthy and stinking. At night we were turned out of the boat into a village—the name I forget, and I would not write it if I remembered. It nearly made an end of me. There were sixty of us to sup together in the tavern, a medley of human animals in one small heated room. It was ten o'clock, and, oh! the dirt and the noise, especially after the wine had begun to circulate. The cries of the boatmen woke us in the morning. I hurry on board unsupped and unslept. At nine we reached Strasburg, when things mended a little. . . . From Strasburg we went on to Speyer. . . . My English horse had broken down, a wretch of a blacksmith having burnt his foot with a hot shoe. I escaped the inn at Speyer and was entertained by my friend the Dean. Two pleasant days with him, thence in a carriage to Worms and so on to Mentz, where I was again lodged by a Cathedral canon. So far things have gone tolerably with me. The smell of the horses was disagreeable and the pace was slow. But that was the worst. At a village further on I called on my friend Christopher, the wine merchant, to his great delight. On his table I saw the works of Erasmus. He invited a party to meet me, sent the boatmen a pitcher of wine and promised to let them off the customs duty as a reward for having brought him so great a man! Thence to Bonn. Thence to Cologne which we reached early on Sunday morning.

Imagine a wine merchant reading my books and given to the study of the Muses. Christ said the publicans and harlots would go into the kingdom of heaven before the Pharisees. Priests and monks live for their bellies, and vintners take to literature! But, alas, the red wine which he sent to the boatmen took the taste of the bargeman's wife, a red-faced sot of a woman. She drank it to the last drop, and then flew to arms and almost murdered a servant wench with oyster shells. Then she rushed on deck, tackled her husband, and tried to pitch him over-board. There is vinal energy for you!

After describing some misadventures at Cologne and a pleasant visit of five days at the home of the Count of New Eagle near that city, Erasmus continues:

The night was wild. I rose before dawn to finish off some work. The Count protested that I must not leave his house in such weather. I must have lost half of my mind when I went to Cologne. My evil genius now carried off the other half. Go I would in an open carriage, with the wind enough to tear up oak trees. It came from the south and was charged with pestilence. Towards evening wind changed to rain. I reached Aix shaken to pieces by the bad roads. I should have done better on my lame horse. At Aix a canon to whom the Count had recommended me carried me off to the house of the Precentor to sup. Other Cathedral dignitaries were also of the party. My light breakfast had sharpened my appetite and there was nothing to eat but cold carp. I filled myself as I could, and went early to bed under the plea that I had not slept the night before. Next day I was taken to the Vice-Provost, whose table usually was well provided, but on this occasion, owing to the weather, he had nothing to offer but eels. These I could not touch, and I had to fall back on salt cod, called "bacalao," from the sticks they beat it with. It was almost raw. Breakfast over, I returned to the inn and ordered a fire. The canon stayed an hour and a half talking. My stomach then went into a crisis. . . .

Another wild night. Breakfast in the morning, a mouthful of bread and a cup of warm beer, and then to my lame beast. I ought to have been in bed, but I dislike Aix and its ways and longed to be off. . . . After a few miles we came to the bridge over the Meuse where I had some broth, and thence on to Tongres. The pain then grew horrible. I would have walked, but I was afraid of perspiring or being out after nightfall. I reached Tongres very ill all over. I slept, however, a little, had some warm beer again in the morning and ordered a closed carriage. The road turned out to be paved with flint. I could not bear the jolting and mounted one of the horses. A sudden chill, and I fainted, and was put back into the carriage. After a while I recovered a little and again tried to ride. In the evening I was sick and told the driver I would pay him double if he would bring me early to my next stage. A miserable night—suffering dreadful. In the morning I found there was a carriage with four horses going straight through to Louvain. I engaged it and arrived the next night in an agony of pain. Fearing that my rooms would be cold, I drove to the house of my kind friend Theodoric, the printer. An ulcer broke in the night and I was easier. I send for a surgeon. He finds another on my back, glands swollen and boils forming all over me. He tells Theodoric's servant that I have the plague, and that he will not come near me again. . . . I send the doctors to the devil, commend myself to Christ, and am well in three days. Who could believe that this frail body of mine could have borne such a shaking? When I was young I was greatly afraid of dying, but I fear it less as I grow older.

The foregoing extracts are enough to indicate that Erasmus was a master of the rare and fine art of letter writing. His correspondence with his friends forms the most voluminous part of all his literary remains. From the days of Pliny to those of our own Walter Hines Page, no one has surpassed him in the field of epistolary literature. His accomplished American biographer justly says: ''For the lover of history and of good literature Erasmus's Epistles are a feast. He serves up all his own sweet and reasonable ideas, many a lively anecdote, and not a few exquisite portraits, with the sauce of gentle humour and the warmth of a facile, charming, if not classical, Latin. And what a society one meets at his hospitable board! Popes and monarches, nobles and bankers, reformers, scholars, artists, writers, Luther, Melancthon, Margaret of Navarre, Colet, More, Budé, Zwingli, Oecolampadius,

Alexander, Rabelais! But to name them all would be to call the roll of half the great men of the early Sixteenth Century."[1]

But letter writing was not the only forte of Erasmus. His *Adages*, a collection of wise say-ings, his *Colloquies*, a series of dialogues on current questions of manners, morals, and cus-toms, and his *Praise of Folly*, a satire on po-litical and ecclesiastical hypocrisy, warrant the assertion that he is one of the earliest as well as one of the greatest of the founders of modern literature. A biting arraignment of papal world-liness in the form of a dialogue at the gate of heaven between Pope Julius II, his Familiar Spirit and St. Peter is ascribed to him, although he neither admitted nor denied its authorship. In this amusing but audacious skit, Julius is made to appear at the entrance to Paradise and to demand admission. Peter subjects him to an examination in which the spiritual and physi-cal vices of some of the pre-Reformation popes are frankly and picturesquely exposed. Julius naïvely assumes that his worldly success, his riches and his temporal power entitle him to admission without any impudent cross exami-nation. Peter says, No, and the lively contro-versy ends as follows:

Julius. Then you won't open the gates?

Peter. Sooner to anyone than such as you. We are not of your communion in this place. You have an army of sturdy rogues behind you, you have money, and you are a famous architect. Go build a Paradise of your own, and fortify it, lest the devils break in on you.

Julius. I will do better than that. I will wait a few months till I have a larger force, and then if you don't give in I will take your place by storm. They are making fine havoc just now. I shall soon have sixty thousand ghosts behind me.

Peter. Oh, wretched man! Oh, miserable church! You, Spirit, I must speak with you; I can say no more to this monster. Are the bishops generally like this one?

Spirit. A good part of them. But he is the top, far and away.

Peter. Was it you who tempted him to commit all these crimes?

Spirit. Not I. He went too fast. I must have had wings to keep abreast of him.

Peter. I am not surprised that so few apply here now for admission, when the Church has such rulers. Yet there must be good in the world, too, when such a sink of iniquity can be honoured, merely because he bears the name of Pope.

Spirit. That is the real truth. But my master beckons to me and lifts his stick. Adieu!

Later historians have handled Julius more gingerly. A professor of history in Columbia University and author of the article on Julius in the Encyclopædia Britannica says:

Julius is deserving of particular honour for his patronage of art and literature. He did much to improve and beautify Rome; he laid the foundation stone of St. Peter's; he founded the Vatican museum; he was a friend and patron of Bramante, Raphael, and Michelangelo. While moderate in personal expenditure, Julius resorted to objectionable means of replenishing the papal treasury, which had been exhausted by Alexander VI, and of providing funds for his numerous enterprises; simony and traffic in indulgences were increasingly prevalent. Julius was undoubtedly, in energy and genius, one of the greatest popes since Innocent III, and it is a misfortune of the Church that his temporal policy eclipsed his spiritual office.

Misfortune indeed! thought Erasmus. His interpretation of the degrading character of that misfortune may be found in the Julian dialogue which is printed in full in Froude's *Life and Letters of Erasmus*. Those who read it there will share my wonder that it did not lead to excommunication. Perhaps its authorship could not be fastened upon him, although Rome was not exacting in those days about the quality of testimony which it brought against its accused.

The satire which Erasmus employed in exposing the vices of the ecclesiastical establishment brought down upon his head a storm of criticism. He felt it necessary to write a long letter of apology and explanation to an old friend and university mate at Louvain, "the excellent theologian," as Erasmus calls him, Martin Dorpius or Van Dorp. In this letter Erasmus asserts that he has never knowingly attacked any individual or blackened a single reputation.

I write not [he asserts] what my enemies deserve but what I must to preserve my own self respect. Moreover, I have no enemy so hateful that I do not hope some day to make a friend of him. Why deprive myself of the chance? Why blacken the character of one whom I can never again make spotless even though he should in future win my approbation? I would rather be mistaken in praising people who do not deserve praise than in censuring those who do not deserve censure.[1]

Although the satire of Erasmus was Voltairean in its thrust and keenness, unlike Voltaire, he had a truly pious and constructive side. He ardently believed in a simple and reasonable Christianity. As his contribution to its promotion he translated, annotated, and paraphrased the New Testament, saying:

I vehemently dissent from those who would not have private persons read the Holy Scriptures nor have them translated into the vulgar tongues, as though either Christ taught such difficult doctrines that they can only be understood by a few theologians, or safety of the Christian religion lay in ignorance of it. I should like all women to read the Gospel and the Epistles of Paul. Would that they were translated into all languages so that not only Scotch and Irish, but Turks and Saracens might be able to read and know them.[2]

---

[1] From Victor Develay's French version of the *Praise of Folly*.
[2] Preserved Smith.

This popularization of the New Testament alone makes Erasmus a benefactor of mankind, Mark Pattison, the great Rector of Lincoln College, Oxford, and himself a clergyman of an established church, says:

Of Erasmus's works the Greek Testament is the most memorable. It has no title to be considered as a work of learning or scholarship, yet its influence upon opinion was profound and durable. It contributed more to the liberation of the human mind from the thraldom of the clergy than all the uproar and rage of Luther's many pamphlets.

Erasmus cannot be said to have been a happy man. In all his seventy years he had scarcely one friendship that did not bring him grief. His capacity for fine friendships is revealed in what he said of the Swiss printer, Froben, with whom he was closely associated for ten years:

Who would not love such a nature? He was to his friends the one best friend, so simple and sincere that even if he had wished to pretend or conceal anything he could not have done it, so repugnant was it to his nature. He was so ready and eager to help everyone that he was glad to be of service even to the unworthy, and thus became a fit prey to thieves and swindlers. He was as pleased to get back money stolen or lent to a fraudulent debtor as others are with an unexpected fortune. His incorruptible honour deserved the saying: "He was a man you could trust to play fair in the dark." Incapable of fraud him-

self, he could never see it in others, though he was not
seldom deceived. He could no more imagine the disease
of envy than a man born blind can understand colours.
He pardoned even serious offences before he asked who
committed them. He could never remember an injury
nor forget the smallest service.[1]

The heart of Erasmus was bound to England
by close ties. When Sir Thomas More was be-
headed by Henry VIII the black tragedy robbed
Erasmus of two friends—the king whom in
youth he had admired as a liberal and who had
now become a bloody despot, and More whose
soul he said he loved as if it were his own. He
lived in a time of surge and revolution and, like
all moderate men who strive to avoid bitterness
and violence in such times of crisis, was battered
by progressives and reactionaries alike. He
suffered all his life not only from spiritual but
from physical irritations which might, not un-
naturally, have made him a cynic and a pessimist.
But he died, a priest of the church he had done
so much to purify, with touching expressions of
his trust in God.

Erasmus was a man of culture rather than of
spiritual power, although he appreciated and admired spiritual ideals, as his friendship for Sir
Thomas More and Dean Colet testifies. No

---

[1]Preserved Smith.

man can estimate the influence which Erasmus has exerted upon the higher life of mankind, because no man can estimate the unseen and immeasurable influence which passes, unnoted by the world, from the printed page to the soul and mind of the reader. And Erasmus stood first, last, and all the time for giving man free access to the printed page. He did not and would not admit the limitations of sex, or creed, or riches, or poverty, or office, or power, within the Republic of Letters. He was a champion of the democracy of books. By everyone who finds nourishment, enlightenment, or solace in literature, he deserves to be canonized as the great emancipator of the intellect.

VOLTAIRE

❖

THE HUMANITARIAN

HE HUMANITARIAN

BORN 1694—DIED 1778

VOLTAIRE had two things in common with his patron saint, Francis of Assisi— he disappointed his father and thwarted that worthy's plans for his career, and late in life he developed a great humanitarian spirit. His father, a modest member of the legal profession, wished the boy to be a lawyer. The boy, when still very young, determined to be a man of letters. "Literature," sniffed the father, "is a profession which is likely to make a man useless to society, a burden to his relatives, and to reduce him finally to starvation," and offered to buy his son a successful law practice. "Tell my father," retorted the son, "that I do not want a bought position; I prefer to make one for myself that shall cost nothing." This he proceeded to do, but by methods which cost him friendships, reputation, health, and more than once put his life in jeopardy.

He created not only a position but literally

a name for himself. His family name was Arouet; his baptismal names were François Marie. The name Voltaire he assumed. Some say it is an anagram arranged out of *Arouet le jeune;* some that it is a diminutive of *le petit volontaire*, a nickname applied to him in childhood because he was so self-willed; some that it was the name of certain remote maternal ancestors. Whatever its derivation, it was a happy choice. It is brief, euphonious, and easily pronounced. English-speaking persons cannot mangle it as they sometimes do the name of Goethe and as they doubtless would have mangled Voltaire's natural patronymic. Here only an outline of his biography can be given; for its romantic and tragic details the reader is referred to S. G. Tallentyre, or to Richard Aldington; for a more serious and philosophical interpretation of Voltaire's life and influence, to John Morley.

Although he was to become the arch-critic of the Catholic Church, Voltaire was educated in a Jesuit College, where he was a brilliant student. Somewhat difficult to manage, he was sent, when about twenty years of age, as a kind of diplomatic attaché to Holland, where he had his first, slightly scandalous and probably only genuine, love affair. Returning to Paris, he

created a furor by his brilliant wit and was
thrown into the Bastille because of an audacious
political pamphlet. On his release, his epigrams
involved him in a quarrel with the Chevalier de
Rohan, a haughty aristocrat, who caused him to
be beaten by the Rohan lackeys and then to be
thrown into the Bastille a second time. From
this dungeon he was released on condition that
he would leave France. He went to England
where he learned her language, and made acquaintance with some of her notable literary
personages, among them that other great satirist,
Dean Swift. Returning to Paris at the age of
thirty-five, he wrote some of his famous plays,
his history of Charles XII, and his *Lettres
Philosophiques* in which he attacked the current
opinions of philosophy, politics, and religion.
Parliament ordered these letters to be burnt by
the public executioner and Voltaire had to escape into Lorraine where he formed an association with Madame du Chatelet, with whom he
lived for ten years on queer terms of intimacy
and antagonism. It was not her beauty, for she
had none, but her intellect, for she was a scientist
and a mathematician, which attracted him. He
was as loyal to her as if he had married her—
perhaps even more so. She finally died in
childbirth, and nobody seems to be quite sure

whether the father of the baby was her husband, Voltaire, or another lover, a poetical young officer who lived for a time in the abnormal menagerie. Madame du Chatelet having died and Voltaire having made his peace with the Paris authorities, he accepted the invitation of Frederick the Great to join the latter's court in Berlin.

Voltaire's life at the court of Frederick does not make a pleasant story. It was brilliant and occasionally splendid. But it was artificial, and its professed love of intellectual genius, and of poetry and letters, was tainted by petty jealousies and dissipation. It ended in a bitter quarrel with Frederick, and Voltaire fled with difficulty into France. The last years of his life he dwelt with a niece at Ferney, near Geneva, where he did not cease to protest against political and ecclesiastical despotism wherever it showed its head. Here he lived as a kind of intellectual monarch receiving visitors from all parts of Europe who came to pay their respects to the champion of free thought and free speech. When eighty-four, he returned for a visit to Paris, where he was hailed by both masses and classes as the great Genius of France. The Paris visit was too much for the worn-out old man, and its excitements resulted in his death.

Although just three months before his death he
had written to a friend, "I die revering God,
helping my friends, forgiving my enemies, and
detesting superstition," the Archbishop of Paris
forbade the burial of his body with the ritual
of the Church. But his relatives outwitted the
Archbishop, and the remains of Voltaire were
laid away hastily and secretly at the abbey of
Scellières, near Paris, with full ecclesiastical
rites, before the prior—a relative of Voltaire—
had received the Archbishop's orders. Thus
sadly ended one of the saddest but most eventful
lives in literary history.

When I was a boy in New England the name of
Voltaire was almost unmentionable in polite
society. He was regarded as the arch-enemy of
all that is good in the universe—the very personi-
fication of Milton's Satan "hurled headlong
flaming from the ethereal sky" to "make a
heaven of hell, a hell of heaven." Like the
mediæval Christian who used to make the sign
of the cross whenever the name of the devil was
uttered, so the orthodox New Englander shud-
dered and metaphorically crossed himself at the
very thought of Voltaire. In his case the old
adage, *de mortuis nil nisi bonum*, was reversed
and nothing was imagined or spoken of him but
evil. He was not respectable, which is the worst

thing that can be said of a man in a society of conventional morals. Naturally, I breathed in this commonly accepted estimate from the atmosphere, and I can well remember the time when I should have thought it extremely hazardous to read any of his wicked writings. Even now I have not read much of them, for his collected works fill seventy volumes. But I have read enough—the *Remarks on Pascal*, the *Philosophical Letters*, *Candide*, *L'Ingénu*, the *Life of Charles XII*, and some of the poems, for example —so that my views about him have undergone a radical change.

Voltaire is certainly to be classed, not only among the great men of letters, but among the great liberators of the human mind, although he was far from being one of the noblest and most admirable of the band. What that fine and open-minded critic John Morley—or, to use his final cognomen Lord Morley—says of Voltaire appears to me to sum up most truly his work and influence: "When the right sense of historical proportion is more fully developed in men's minds, the name of Voltaire will stand out like the names of the great decisive movements in the European advance, like the Revival of Learning, or the Reformation," although, as Lord Morley admits, he often "offends two modern sentiments, the love of modesty, and the love of the heroic personages of history."

In his *Outline of History*, Mr. H. G. Wells—himself not a highly reverential person—brushes aside the great French rationalist as "that supreme mocker, Voltaire." This is a superficial judgment. It is probably true that Voltaire, in the prodigious quantity of his writings, employed mockery more than any other literary genius of history, not even excepting George Bernard Shaw! But Voltaire used mockery as a means, not an end, which can hardly be said of the author of *Back to Methuselah*. Lord Morley's comment on the use of mockery by Voltaire is more to the point:

Let us not forget that what Catholicism was accomplishing in France in the first half of the Eighteenth Century, was really not anything less momentous than the slow strangling of French civilization. Though Voltaire's spirit may be little edifying to us, who after all partake of the freedom which he did so much to win, yet it is only just to remember what was the spirit of his foe, and that in so pestilent a presence a man of direct vision may well be eager to use such weapons as he finds to his hands. Let the scientific spirit move people to speak as it lists about Voltaire's want of respect for things held sacred, for the good deeds of holy men, for the sentiment and faith of thousands of the most worthy among his fellows. Still there are times when it may be very questionable whether, in the region of belief, one with power and with fervid honesty ought to spare the abominable city of the plain, just because it happens to shelter five righteous.

So far from being an habitual mocker of what is good, beautiful, and true, Voltaire often displayed a spirit of simple tenderness and genuine reverence. In *L'Ingénu* or *The Innocent*, a fantastic tale of a supposed young Huron Indian who is cast upon the shores of France and cannot understand the theological intricacies or social conventions of the sophisticated and artificial society in which he is plunged, there is a charming and touching love story which puts the relations of the sexes on the highest plane. And the portrait of the Jansenist Gordon, drawn in swift but vivid strokes, is admirable. It is true that Voltaire uses some of the characters of this story to satirize delicately and delightfully the follies of the French church and French society, just as H. G. Wells, in *The Wonderful Visit*, tells the story of an angel's life in England to ridicule certain phases of English social conditions and of the Church of England. But it is not all mockery in the case of either story-teller.

Voltaire is often called an atheist. This epithet is wholly unjust. In his comments on the *Pensées* of Pascal he clearly indicates his belief in a Divine Power in the universe. Pascal had said that when he saw the blind misery of mankind, living on earth as if on a desert island, without knowing whence they had come or whither they were going, he wondered that the human race did not fall into black despair in thinking of its wretched state. To this pessimism Voltaire replied as follows:

What wise man would fall into despair because he does not understand the nature of thought or the attributes of matter, or because God has not revealed His secrets to him? Man might as well despair because he has not got four feet and two wings. Why should life fill us with horror? Our existence is not as miserable as some would have us believe. To look upon the universe as a jail and all men as criminals who are on their way to execution is the notion of a fanatic; to believe that the world is a place of mere delight in which one has nothing to do but to pursue pleasure is the fantasy of a sybarite; the wise man, it seems to me, will look upon the earth, its men, and its animal creatures as the product of a divine plan.

Again Pascal complains:

It must be admitted that man is so wretched that he is bored by his own existence without any external cause of boredom.

And again Voltaire replies:

Would it not also be true to say that we are under such obligations to the Creator that He has made ennui a product of laziness so as to force us by that very fact to be useful to our neighbours and ourselves?

Once more Pascal deplores the hopelessness of life in a simile:

> The rudder guides those on shipboard, but where shall we find such a guide in the sea of morals?

And once more Voltaire answers cheerfully:

> In the simple maxim, the truth of which is accepted by all men, *Do not do to another what you would not have that other do to you.*

A mere mocker could not have written these things. It is true that Voltaire did not always practise what he preached, but it is equally true that he often preached what it is good to practise.

I am not, however, recommending Voltaire as a moralist; those who are interested in the history of literature and in the progress of civilization ought to make his acquaintance on other grounds. He should be read, or some of his work should be read—for much of it is inferior or obsolete—as the product of one of the great men of letters. His *métier* was not limited. He ventured into every field of literature, more so, perhaps, than any other first-rate writer of modern times. He tried his hand at history, biography, poetry, drama, fiction, science, theology, metaphysics, and criticism. An envious rival once said that he could write anything to order like an encyclopædia-hack. Nevertheless, in all that he wrote, the precision of his style is a model and his wit is sparkling, often stinging a little, as sparks usually do. He was a master of the rhymed epigram and used that weapon to rout his enemies, for he made enemies as easily and enjoyed them as much as Whistler did. One of his contemporaries and antagonists was the celebrated critic Fréron, whom he liked to handle without gloves, as the following epigram shows:

> L'autre jour, au fond d'un vallon,
> Un serpent piqua Jean Fréron.
> Que pensez-vous qu'il arriva?
> Ce fut le serpent qui creva.

Or, as it might be put into English:

> The other day beside a valley lake,
> Poor Jean Fréron was bitten by a snake
> But weep not, Reader, let your grief subside,
> 'Twas not Fréron but the poor snake that died.

Another epigram was aimed at a contemporary, a would-be man of letters, a type for which Voltaire had a great contempt. This was Jacques Lefranc, the Marquis de Pompignan, who wrote a tragedy and some "sacred poems" which Voltaire said were "sacred because nobody touched them." Lefranc's literary output was of about the quality to be expected from a nobleman who thinks that a title may give him the place at the literary table which genius has denied him.   Nobody would recall Lefranc's name to-day if it were not for Voltaire's epigrammatic wit:

> Savez-vous pourquoi Jérémie
> A tant pleuré pendant sa vie?
> C'est qu'en prophète il prévoyait
> Qu'un jour Lefranc le traduirait.

This might read in rhymed English:

> Jeremiah's anger was so free,
>   So low and sad a view of life he took,
> Because, as prophet he could well foresee
>   Lefranc's translation of his precious book.

Voltaire furnishes a good example of the folly of answering petty contemporary critics. Most of his enemies during his lifetime, to use the words of Macaulay,

were, indeed, contemptible assailants. Of all that they wrote against him, nothing has survived except what he himself preserved. But the constitution of his mind resembled the constitution of those bodies in which the slightest scratch of a bramble, or the bite of a gnat, never fails to fester. Though his reputation was rather raised than lowered by the abuse of such writers as Fréron and Desfontaines, though the vengeance which he took on Fréron and Desfontaines was such that scourging, branding, pillorying, would have been a trifle to it, there is reason to believe that they gave him far more pain than he ever gave them.

As a stylist, Voltaire is in the very front rank of all times and all languages. His own receipt for the cultivation of style is found in a letter which he wrote when an "old invalid"—so he called himself—to a young lady who asked his advice:

Reading our best poets is better than all lessons. . . . Read only such books as have long been sealed with the universal approval of the public and whose reputation is established. They are few, but you will gain much more from reading those few than from all the feeble little works with which we are inundated. . . . The smallest affectation is a vice. . . . Observe how naturally Madame de Sévigné and other ladies write, and compare their style with the confused phrases of our minor romancers—I cite writers of your own sex because I am sure you can, and will, resemble them. . . . You will notice that our good writers—Fénelon, Boussuet, Racine, Despreaux—always use the right word. One gets oneself accustomed to talk well by constantly reading those who have written well; it becomes a habit to express our thoughts simply and nobly without an effort. It is not in the nature of a study; it is no trouble to read what is good, and to read that only; our own pleasure and taste are our only masters.

These literary principles are followed by Voltaire not only in his lighter writing but in his serious work. Carlyle declared the *Life of*

Charles XII to be a model of biographical writing. In his opinion it is written

in a style which for graphic brevity rivals Sallust. It is a line engraving on a reduced scale of that Swede and his mad life, without colours, yet not without the foreshortenings and perspectives of a true picture. In respect of composition . . . we cannot but reckon it as greatly the best of Voltaire's histories.

Macaulay thought it comparable to Boswell's *Johnson*. It is only fair to say, however, that Macaulay, with the characteristic moral standards of the British Whig, thoroughly disliked Voltaire. As a historian, he appreciated Voltaire's historical gifts; as a moralist, he could not refrain from satirizing his ethics. He describes Voltaire's critical prose as a mixture of

much lively and picturesque narrative, many and just and humane sentiments poignantly expressed, many grotesque blunders, many sneers at the Mosaic chronology, much scandal about the Catholic missionaries, and much sublime theo-philanthropy, stolen from the New Testament, and put into the mouths of virtuous and philosophical Brahmins.

Nowhere does Voltaire's mastery of style appear more clearly than in his letters. They suffer, as all idiosyncratic writing does, from translation. Nevertheless, a selection of them has been rendered into English as well as they

cān be by Tallentyre. From his volume I
choose one as an illustration not only of Voltaire's
style but of his wisdom. It was written to a
government official as a protest against what
Lord Morley called "the slow strangling of
French civilization":

As you have it in your power, Sir, to do some service to
letters, I implore you not to clip the wings of our writers
so closely, nor to turn into barn-yard fowls those who,
allowed a start, might become eagles; reasonable liberty
permits the mind to soar—slavery makes it creep.

Had there been a literary censorship in Rome, we should
have had to-day neither Horace, Juvenal, nor the philosophical works of Cicero. If Milton, Dryden, Pope and
Locke had not been free, England would have had neither
poets nor philosophers; there is something positivelyTurk-
ish in proscribing printing; and hampering it *is* proscrip-
tion. Be content with severely repressing defamatory
libels, for they are crimes; but as long as infamous epigrams are boldly published, and so many other unworthy
and despicable productions, at least allow Bayle [an
influential philosophical and literary critic who was persecuted and repressed by the government] to circulate in
France, and do not put him who has been so great an
honour to his country among its contraband.

You say that the magistrates who regulate the literary
customhouse complain that there are too many books.
That is just the same thing as if the provost of merchants
complained there were too many provisions in Paris.
People buy what they choose. A great library is like the
City of Paris, in which there are about eight hundred
thousand persons; you do not live with the whole crowd;
you choose a certain society, and change it. So with

books; you choose a few friends out of the many. There will be seven or eight thousand controversial books, and fifteen or sixteen thousand novels, which you will throw into the fire after you have read them. The man of taste will read only what is good; but the statesman will permit both bad and good.

Men's thoughts have become an important article of commerce. The Dutch publishers make a million francs a year, because Frenchmen have brains. A feeble novel is, I know, among books what a fool, always striving after wit, is in the world. We laugh at him and tolerate him. Such a novel brings the means of life to the author who wrote it, the publisher who sells it, to the stereotyper, the printer, the paper-maker, the binder, the carrier—and finally to the bad wine-shop where they all take their money. Further, the book amuses for an hour or two a few women who like novelty in literature as in everything. Thus, despicable though it may be, it will have produced two important things—profit and pleasure.

The theatre also deserves attention. I do not consider it a counter attraction to dissipation; that is a notion only worthy of an ignorant curé. . . . I look on tragedy and comedy as lessons in virtue, good sense and good behaviour. Corneille—the old Roman of the French—has founded a school of Spartan virtue; Molière, a school of ordinary, everyday life. These great national geniuses attract foreigners from all parts of Europe, who come to study among us, and thus contribute to the wealth of Paris. Our poor are fed by the production of such works, which bring under our rule the very nations which hate us. In fact, he who condemns the theatre is an enemy to his country. A magistrate who, because he has succeeded in buying some judicial post, thinks that it is beneath his dignity to see *Cinna* [one of the greatest of Corneille's tragedies] shows much pomposity and very little taste.

There are still Goths and Vandals even among our cultivated people; the only Frenchmen I consider worthy of the name are those who love and encourage the arts. It is true that the taste for them is languishing; we are sybarites, weary of our mistresses' favours. . . . Nothing will rouse us from this indifference to great things which always goes side by side with our vivid interest in small.

Every year we take more pains over snuff boxes and nicknacks than the English took to make themselves masters of the seas. . . . The old Romans raised these marvels of architecture—their amphitheatres—for beasts to fight in; and for a whole century we have not built a single passable place for the representation of the masterpieces of the human mind. A hundredth part of the money spent on cards would be enough to build theatres finer than Pompey's; but what man in Paris has the public welfare at heart? We play, sup, talk scandal, write bad verses, and sleep, like fools, to recommence on the morrow the same round of careless frivolity.

You, Sir, who have at least some small opportunity of giving good advice, try and arouse us from this stupid lethargy, and, if you can, do something for literature, which has done so much for France.

Other letters disclose Voltaire's capacity for deeper feeling. Softened by the death of an older sister, for whom he had a tender affection, he wrote an understanding letter of consolation to a friend, also in bereavement, in which he said:

The squaring of the circle and perpetual motion are simple discoveries in comparison to the secret of bringing peace to a soul distraught by passionate grief. It is only

magicians who pretend to calm storms with words. . . .
It depends, I believe, on ourselves to break the links which
bind us to our sorrows and to strengthen those which
attach us to happier things. Not, indeed, that we are
absolute slaves; and, once again, I believe that the Supreme Being has given us a little of His liberty, as He has
given us a little of His power of thought.

The Lisbon earthquake profoundly depressed
Voltaire, but he could not let it pass without
taking the occasion to attack ecclesiastical
despotism. Of it he wrote:

This is indeed a cruel piece of natural philosophy!
. . . What a game of chance human life is! What
will the preachers say—especially if the Palace of the
Inquisition is left standing? I flatter myself that these
reverend fathers, the Inquisitors, must have been crushed
just like other people. That ought to teach men not to
persecute men; for, while a few sanctimonious humbugs
are burning a few fanatics, the earth opens and swallows
up all alike.

When the English Admiral, John Byng, was
unjustly and malevolently sentenced to be shot
because of his defeat by the French fleet under
the Duke of Richelieu, a British friend of Byng's
went all the way to Geneva to beg Voltaire to
intercede. The resulting letters from Voltaire
and Richelieu were fruitless, but their letters and
their efforts are highly creditable to the two
Frenchmen. Voltaire was so incensed by the

crime of Byng's execution that he satirized it in a famous passage in *Candide*. The hero of that satirical masterpiece crosses the Channel and disembarks at Portsmouth.

A crowd of people were standing on the shore and gazing spellbound at a rather big man who, with eyes bandaged, was kneeling on the deck of a warship. Four soldiers stationed face to face with this man, each fired three bullets into his head in the most peaceful fashion imaginable. The crowd dispersed highly satisfied. "What in the world is this," thought Candide. "What Devil rules this place!" On asking a bystander who the big man was whom they had just killed so ceremoniously, the man replied that it was an admiral. "And why kill this admiral?" queried Candide. "Because," was the reply, "he himself did not kill enough other people; he yielded in a naval battle with a French admiral, and the court found that he did not get near enough the Frenchman." "But," protested Candide, "the French admiral was as far away from the English admiral as the English admiral was from the French admiral." "Perfectly true," was the response; "but here in England it is useful once in a while to kill an admiral in order to encourage the others—*pour encourager les autres.*"

Voltaire's humanitarianism was not a matter of the closet or the inkstand. At Ferney he established a model community, promoted agriculture and manufactures, and ameliorated injustices of taxation. He successfully defended several innocent persons from cruel punishments and even death. In one case, he worked for three years, and in another, nine, with tooth and nail, before he finally succeeded in saving the victims in these cases from the vengeance of bigotry and despotism. This phase of his career well entitles him to be called, as Tallentyre calls him, Humanitarian-in-Chief of Europe.

The modification of the judgment pronounced on Voltaire by the pious and intellectual world of his day and of our own is striking. His contemporaries admired and feared his wit and intellectual power but destested his principles and personality. What respectable Europe thought of him is crystallized in a story told by Matthew Arnold of the poet Thomas Gray, author of the famous "Elegy":

Voltaire's literary genius charmed him, but the faults of Voltaire's nature he felt so strongly that when his young friend Nicholls was going abroad in 1771, just before Gray's death, he said to him: "I have one thing to beg of you which you must not refuse." Nicholls answered: "You know you have only to command; what is it?"— "Do not go to see Voltaire," said Gray; and then added: "No one knows the mischief that man will do." Nicholls promised compliance with Gray's injunction; "But what," he asked, "could a visit from me signify?"—"Every tribute to such a man signifies," Gray answered.

Now, Gray was a Cambridge Fellow and, by education, a clergyman of the Church of England. He shared the moral sentiments and prejudices of his class and his time. But seventy or eighty years later, another clergyman of the Church of England, Jowett of Balliol, one of the finest figures produced by Oxford, not only expressed admiration for Voltaire's wit and style but once remarked that "civilization owes more to Voltaire than to all the Fathers of the Church put together." Still more striking is the judgment of W. E. H. Lecky, whose *Rise and Influence of Rationalism in Europe* made a literary sensation when it was first published in 1865. Lecky, by the way, was educated for the Church and is one of the best equipped and fairest-minded of English historians. A passage in his defense of rationalism is an eloquent defense of simple Christianity which is worth reading for the beauty of its style if for nothing else:

If it be true Christianity to dive with a passionate charity into the darkest recesses of misery and of vice, to irrigate every quarter of the earth with the fertilizing stream of an almost boundless benevolence, and to include all the sections of humanity in the circle of an intense and efficacious sympathy; if it be true Christianity to destroy or weaken the barriers which had separated class from class and nation from nation, to free war from its harshest elements, and to make a consciousness of essential equality and of a genuine fraternity dominate over all accidental differences; if it be, above all, true Christianity to cultivate a love of truth for its own sake, a spirit of candour and of tolerance towards those with whom we differ—if these be the marks of a true and healthy Christianity, then never since the days of the Apostles has it been so vigorous as at present, and the decline of dogmatic systems and of clerical influence has been a measure if not a cause of its advance.

The man who wrote the foregoing noble interpretation of Christianity wrote the following memorable judgment of Voltaire:

Voltaire was at all times the unflinching opponent of persecution. No matter how powerful was the persecutor, no matter how insignificant was the victim, the same scathing eloquence was launched against the crime, and the indignation of Europe was soon concentrated upon the oppressor. The fearful storm of sarcasm and invective that avenged the murder of Calas, the magnificent dream in the *Philosophical Dictionary* reviewing the history of persecution from the slaughtered Canaanites to the latest victims who had perished at the stake, the indelible stigma branded upon the persecutors of every age and of every creed, all attested the intense and passionate earnestness with which Voltaire addressed himself to his task. On other subjects a jest or a caprice could often turn him aside. When attacking intolerance, he employed, indeed, every weapon, but he employed them all with the concentrated energy of a profound conviction. His success was equal to his zeal. The spirit of intolerance sank blasted beneath his genius. Wherever his influence passed the arm of the Inquisitor was palsied, the chain of the captive riven, the prison door flung open. Beneath his withering irony persecution appeared not only criminal but loathsome, and since his time it has ever shrunk from observation, and masked its features under other names. He died, leaving a reputation that is indeed far

from spotless, but having done more to destroy the greatest of human curses than any other of the sons of men.

Voltaire was a singular combination of the
ancient and the modern—an ancient because he
had all the petty vanities and jealousies of an
Egyptian sorcerer: a modern because he was, in
his conception of moral and political rights and
duties, far in advance of his age. It is not an
exaggeration to say that the history of literature
knows no other such extraordinary bundle of
contradictions. He was mean and noble; a
truth-seeker and an unscrupulous liar; vain and
self-effacing; religious and blasphemous; credulous and sceptical; genuine and artificial; generous and greedy; spiteful and sympathetic; a
lover of luxury and a tireless worker. Half the
time he was fighting personal enemies to satisfy
his own vanity, and half the time he was bravely
attacking prejudice, ignorance, and injustice for
the protection of mankind. In his courage, he
had some of the majesty of the lion, but his
method of attack was to buzz and sting like a
hornet. The good that may be said of him is
that, at a time when ecclesiastical vice and
political injustice prevailed, he sincerely hated
both and fought bigot and tyrant even at the
risk of his own life. It is true that in exposing
the corrupt alliance of church and state he often

brought contempt on all religion and has sometimes been appropriated as their excuse by those who would undermine all authority and order. Nevertheless, by his trenchant criticism he set nobler if less brilliant men thinking on human rights and human freedom and is entitled to respect and admiration as one of the great apostles of the world-wide humanitarian movement that has characterized the Eighteenth and Nineteenth centuries.   For the modern reader he is a kind of moral alcohol—stimulating when taken with discretion but poisonous if gulped down indiscriminately.

THOMAS JEFFERSON

THE ARISTOCRAT

FIVE: THOMAS JEFFERSON

THE ARISTOCRAT

BORN 1743—DIED 1826

PRIVATE WILLIS in "Iolanthe" sings a
song which, in humorous guise, states a
serious philosophical truth. He says that every
British child that's born into the world alive is
either a little Liberal or a little Conservative.
So it may be said that every American child is
born either a Hamiltonian or a Jeffersonian, although those two great statesmen have been
dead for a century. The ardent partisanship of
Revolutionary days clings to their memory.
Jefferson is still the patron saint of those who
think politically in terms of individualism;
Hamilton of those who, in theory at least, subordinate individual and local authority to a
strong and sovereign nationalism—or, as the
followers of Jefferson call it, imperialism.

How widespread this partisanship is and how
emotional its character finds an illustration in
current biographical literature. A few years ago
an Englishman, Mr. F. S. Oliver, a Cambridge

man, wrote a biography of Alexander Hamilton which was widely read on both sides of the Atlantic. It is an able and scholarly work, although it must be admitted that it does scant justice to Jefferson. Recently another Englishman, Francis W. Hirst, a graduate of Oxford and a barrister, has written a life of Jefferson. It is evident that Mr. Hirst was born a little Liberal and Mr. Oliver a little Conserva*tive*. Mr. Hirst, not content with portraying Jefferson, goes out of his way to strike at Mr. Oliver, whose life of Hamilton he calls a "caricature or travesty." Oliver, he asserts, "threw up a cloud of glittering dust around the career of Alexander Hamilton," calls his biography an "overcoloured portrait, painted in the heyday of commercial imperialism by a disciple of Mr. Chamberlain," and contemptuously dismisses it as belonging "to fiction rather than to history." There is something amusing in this spectacle of two Englishmen, representatives of the great rival universities of Great Britain, making a Donnybrook Fair of the field of American politics. It is as if Mr. Bryan and Senator Lodge had belaboured each other with biographies of Gladstone and Disraeli.

When two Englishmen can get so wrought up in a discussion of Jefferson's place in history, it is not surprising that his name should still excite partisan feelings among Americans. For many years in Jefferson's native State of Virginia, the fact that he died on the fiftieth anniversary of the Declaration of Independence—the authorship of which assures Jefferson historic immortality—was considered by his devoted disciples as a special and unique manifestation of the approval of divine Providence. It was almost as if, like Elijah, he had been carried to heavenly bliss in a chariot of fire. Dr. Alderman, of the University of Virginia, tells an amusing story of a good old Virginia Democrat who, when he learned that John Adams, Jefferson's great political rival, died in Boston on the Fourth of July, 1826, a few hours before Jefferson, exclaimed in indignation: "Well, I call it a damned Yankee trick!"

This story is a fair illustration of the passionate differences of opinion that have raged about the name and achievements of the third President of the United States for more than a century. Partisanship, bitter as it was in the lifetime of George Washington, has ceased to play any part in the popular estimation of the Father of his Country. Washington has been adopted without any sectional differences by the whole nation, although when, in March, 1797, he finally left the Presidency, the *Aurora*, the leading news-

paper organ of the Jeffersonian party, announced
that he was about to step into "well-merited
oblivion." But the name of Jefferson is still a
storm centre. It is not surprising that the
philosophy and deeds of his statesmanship have
been too little appreciated by those of a Hamiltonian or nationalistic turn of mind. Jefferson
opposed the judicial power of the Supreme Court;
espoused the policy of States Rights; was the
author of the doctrine of Nullification, which
paved the way for, if it did not actually beget,
the doctrine of Secession; and, although refined,
cultivated, and intellectual in personal tastes and
private life, stooped to some demagogic prac-
tices in political affairs which have given an
unfortunate trend to certain currents of our national history. I confess that I have been swayed
by this nationalistic prejudice against Jefferson,
although I am now ready to admit that in the
reaction against extreme individualism, the
pendulum of American government has swung
too far on the nationalistic side. As will be seen
in the succeeding chapter, John Marshall appears to me to have been, next to Washington,
the greatest of the Fathers of the Republic.
Jefferson's animosity toward Marshall I am
afraid has exasperated and blinded me. That
animosity may, perhaps, be explained, but it

cannot be excused. What thick-and-thin partisans will say to excuse it is found in Hirst's
biography of Jefferson. Here is a university
graduate who took high honours in classics and
literature, who is a lawyer by training, who is
an expert student of economics and history, and
yet who can deliberately say this:

> Marshall was a Federalist politician, who hated the
> French Revolution, and showed his detestation of the
> Republican party by representing their principles as
> hypocrisies, or extravagancies, and their leaders as
> intriguers or imposters. It [Marshall's *Life of Washington*]
> is rather a dull book, but it has an air of historical
> veracity which none knew better [how] to impart than the
> crafty Chief Justice.

Marshall a mere crafty politician who twists
the truth for personal ends! This is almost
enough to make one forswear Jefferson and all
his disciples. But Jefferson ought not to be
made to suffer, as he has so often in political
controversy, from the limitations and laudations
of his over-zealous worshippers. It is customary
to hail him as the great champion of democracy;
he should be honoured as an outstanding exem-
plar of the finest aristocracy—the aristocracy of
intelligence, taste, and manners.

Jefferson was born on his father's farm, or
"estate," of Shadwell, of yeoman ancestry on his

father's side but of aristocratic lineage on his mother's. His mother's family belonged to the squirearchy of England, and one of her family achieved some reputation as a man of letters in the age of Elizabeth. Jefferson himself says that his father's education was self-acquired, but that he improved his mind by much reading. Peter, the father, like Washington and Lincoln, became a surveyor. As the acquisition and partition of land was an important industry in those days, surveying was a lucrative trade or profession. Thus the father became a man of property. Although Peter Jefferson was technically uneducated, he valued education. His library contained some good books and he saw to it that his son had the best schooling obtainable. At school Jefferson studied Greek, Latin, and mathematics, and at seventeen went to William and Mary College. There he became a fair classical scholar well grounded in the French language and its literature, and came to know something of Spanish and Italian. In law he had the training of George Wythe, said to have been the best classical scholar in the Colonies, who also taught John Marshall the rudiments of law. The colony of Virginia, although from the London point of view on the frontier, counted in its population not a few men of British university training.

Jefferson had the advantage of association with some of these men. There was also an element of boisterous, wild, and unrestrained life. Jefferson's social instincts made him popular in both circles. Late in life, in speaking of the gay roisterers with whom he was thrown he said: "I am astonished that I did not turn off with some of them and become as worthless to society as they were." What really protected him was that his tastes were naturally æsthetic and refined. As a boy at Shadwell he had become a first-rate horseman and hunter, but the outdoor life and social gaieties of the colony did not supplant his love of literature and the arts. As a student at the College of William and Mary, he was devoted to music, and said himself that, during a dozen years of his youth, he played on the violin no less than three hours a day. When he became Governor of Virginia, in the third year of the Revolutionary War, he was, as his biographer Parton says, "a lawyer of thirty-six, with a talent for music, a taste for art, a love of science, literature, and gardening."

On leaving college, like any young modern aristocrat who graduates from Harvard, Jefferson did some travelling. He went as far as New York, which was in those days a long and venturesome journey. Returning home, he passed his examinations for the bar and at twenty-four began the practice of his profession. He was successful from the start. In his first year he had sixty-eight cases and his professional income was a handsome one. One biographer says that it averaged three thousand dollars a year, another twelve thousand. Either of these figures was large for the time, and they are measures of his precocious prominence in his profession. As a young man of property, social position, and professional influence, he naturally turned to politics and in 1769 was elected to the House of Burgesses. He was one of the aristocrats of that assembly, as his friend Patrick Henry was one of the democrats. Although speculation in such matters is not especially fruitful, it may be imagined that if the Colonies, like Canada, had remained a part of the British Empire, Jefferson would have developed into a Whig like Macaulay instead of a Radical like John Bright. But the Revolution changed the whole course of his mind and career.

Jefferson never was a successful public speaker, but early won a reputation as a writer of style and of effective, logical argument. In his thirty-second year he wrote the *Summary View* of the quarrel of the Colonies with Great Britain which established on both sides of the Atlantic his position as a political thinker. "Jefferson," says Henry C. Merwin, "was always about a century in advance of his time; and the *Summary View* substantially anticipated what is now the acknowledged relation of England to her colonies." This quality of foresight in Jefferson's grasp of political and social questions appears in a very striking form in the fight which Jefferson led in the House of Burgesses for free men, free speech, and a free church. He advocated the abolition of primogeniture, the gradual suppression of slavery, and the establishment of "full and free liberty of religious opinion." The property-owning class were more incensed by his attack on primogeniture than by his championship of free men and free thought. One of his friends asked him to compromise with the owners of great estates by permitting the eldest son to have a double share of his deceased father's property in land. "Yes," was Jefferson's comment, "when he can eat twice the allowance of food and do double the allowance of work."

Of the greatest political document which Jefferson wrote, the Declaration of Independence, it is not necessary to speak. It speaks for itself. But too much emphasis cannot be laid on the fact that it contains a phrase of eight words which is not surpassed in the whole range of literature as a combination of brevity and moral power—"A decent respect for the opinions of mankind."

Jefferson's democracy was really philanthropy. While living in France as American Minister, he wrote to Lafayette as follows on the practical problems of human welfare: "You must ferret the people out of their hovels as I have done; look into their kettles; eat their bread; loll on their beds on pretense of resting yourself, but in fact to find if they are soft. You will find a sublime pleasure in the course of the investigation, and a sublimer one hereafter, when you shall be able to apply your knowledge to the softening of their beds, or the throwing a morsel of meat into their kettle of vegetables." It was this experience which gave Jefferson a passionate but sometimes one-sided sympathy with the French Revolution, for he ascribed the misery of the French masses wholly to monarchical despotism and taxation.

There is not a crowned head in Europe [he once said to Washington], whose talents of merits would entitle him to be elected a vestryman by the people of America.

But he was not concerned merely with the physical well-being of the masses; he believed, as

Lincoln did later, that the plain people had an innate faculty

which we call common sense; state a moral case to a ploughman and a professor; the former will decide it as well and often better than the latter, because he has not been led astray by artificial rules.

This faith in the common sense or moral sense of the masses he carried to a faulty extreme, but it did not destroy his unconscious instinct for authority. It is not an uncommon custom to contrast the Hamiltonians and the Jeffersonians as Nationalists and Individualists. It is manifest from the records that Jefferson, whatever his theories, was one of the greatest Nationalists of our history. When, in 1786, John Jay, a Hamiltonian, advocated the surrender of the Mississippi to Spanish control, Jefferson wrote to Madison: "The act which abandons it is an act of separation between the eastern and western country." When he became President, he sent Lewis and Clark, with an uncanny premonition of the future growth of the United States, on their memorable expedition through the Northwest to the Pacific coast. Theoretically a pacifist and wishing for a complete separation of the Old World from the New, he advocated a small but efficient navy as a first line of defense, and he put down by force the Barbary pirates of the Mediterranean to whom the European governments, and even his Federalist predecessor, John Adams, had truckled in a cowardly manner. When he effected the Louisiana Purchase, he said that the inhabitants of Louisiana were "as incapable of self-government as children." He himself recognized that the Louisiana Purchase was not quite consistent with his Constitutional theories and wanted the Purchase legalized by a Constitutional amendment. But this was never done. It is a curious coincidence that the two greatest material achievements of our government —the acquisition of the huge Louisiana territory and the building of the Panama Canal—are both suspected of having an extra-Constitutional taint. In the one case, Jefferson pleaded guilty but Congress acquitted him; in the other, Roosevelt insisted upon his clear Constitutional title and Congress smirched it by paying a fine of $25,000,000 to Colombia. In both cases, however, the plain people of the country, exercising the useful faculty of common sense, applaud the acts of President Jefferson and President Roosevelt as long steps in the promotion of human welfare.

Jefferson's political career is, for continuity, the most remarkable in American annals. From the date of his election to the Virginia House of Burgesses in 1769, to his retirement from the Presidency in 1809, is a period of forty years. During this time he held consecutively the most important legislative, diplomatic, and executive offices. There is no record quite like his in our history. He was a shrewd and successful political manager; not even Roosevelt surpassed him in this respect. In many aspects, the political fortunes of Jefferson and Roosevelt were similar. Both began as youthful legislators, both became governors of their respective states, and both served terms as Vice President and as President. But Roosevelt never held the position of Minister Plenipotentiary to a foreign country as Jefferson did in France. Like Roosevelt, Jefferson had his conflicts with Congress. In his second term his party broke away from him over the question of slavery and bitterly disappointed him in its failure to support his carefully laid plans to crush the power of the Supreme Court. I surmise that he may have shared the opinion of Congress held by some of his rivals among the Federalist leaders. What that opinion was appears in an anecdote related by George Pellew in his biography of John Jay:

Congress, in those early days, as pictured in the private correspondence of the French agents and ministers, does not altogether represent that Amphictyonic Council of honourable unselfish patriots into which it has now become transfigured by the magic consecration of time. Some thirty years afterwards [about 1807], Gouverneur Morris was sitting over the polished mahogany at Bedford with John Jay, when he suddenly ejaculated through clouds of smoke, "Jay, what a set of d——d scoundrels we had in that second Congress." "Yes," said Jay, "that we had," and he knocked the ashes from his pipe.

Among all the Revolutionary fathers, Jefferson has an outstanding claim to the title, "A Man of Letters." He was preëminently a scholar in politics—as voracious a reader as Roosevelt and a more voluminous writer than Wilson. Jefferson's father was a reader, being familiar with Shakespeare, Swift, and the *Spectator*. As a college boy, in addition to his studies of Greek, Latin, French, and Anglo-Saxon (into which he delved to discover the sources of the Common Law of England), young Jefferson read Fielding, Smollet, Sterne, Gil Blas, and Cervantes. During his vacations at his country home of Shadwell, he devoted several hours to reading each day in accordance with a regular time table. This scheme of reading is set forth in a memorandum which he prepared when he was twenty-one for Madison and Monroe who were to follow in his footsteps, and which, in 1814, he revised and brought up to date for his grandson. The early

morning hours before eight he dedicates to
"physical studies, namely Agriculture, Chemistry, Anatomy, Zoölogy, Botany." Among the
books on agriculture he names Arthur Young's
Travels in France, a "best seller" of its day,
which fell into desuetude but has been recently
revived as a classic. The hours from eight to
twelve Jefferson devoted to Law and dwelt
upon the value of the case system, in which he
anticipated the methods of modern law teaching.
He advised that Politics should occupy the hour
from twelve to one; here the breadth of his mind
is indicated by his recommendation of *The
Federalist*, the work chiefly of Hamilton, who was
his greatest political antagonist. The afternoon,
thought Jefferson, should be devoted to History,
including Greek and Latin writers in the original,
and Gibbon's Rome. This plan was not the
lucubration of a mere bookworm, for Jefferson,
in addition to being an accomplished man of
outdoor life, an expert horseman, farmer, and
gardener, turned his reading to practical account.
Later in life, in a botanical discussion, he cited,
says Hirst, "Diodorus Siculus and Acosta, the
Spanish authority, on the question whether
maize was known in Europe before the discovery
of America"; and in debating slavery he quoted
"Plutarch, Cato, and Suetonius to prove that

Roman slaves were worse treated than Virginian." When his wife, to whom he was tenderly devoted, died, he inscribed upon her tombstone "the beautiful lines from Achilles' Lament over the dead body of Patroclus in the Iliad."

Jefferson's taste for philosophical discussion, both physical and metaphysical, and his habit of secretive caution, for which he was so much criticized by his political opponents, appear in a remarkable letter that, so far as I can discover, has never before been published. It is now in the possession of John L. Wilkie, Esq., of the New York bar. A relative of his family found and rescued it with other letters, the historical value of which the discoverer understood, from a pile of papers doomed to destruction in a Virginia mansion captured by soldiers of the Union army during the Civil War. The letter itself explains why it bears neither address nor signature, but it has been verified by experts familiar with Jefferson's handwriting. Moreover, there were two others with it in the same well-known handwriting, signed by Jefferson, and the unsigned letter bears an endorsement in faintly pencilled lines, evidently made by the recipient and owner of the mansion or one of his descendants, saying that it was from Jefferson. Mr. Wilkie kindly gives me the privilege of transcribing the letter here.   It was written, as will be seen from the date, in Jefferson's twenty-second year:

Wmsburgh, July 26th, 1764.

I like your proposal of keeping up an epistolary correspondence on subjects of some importance.   I do not at present recollect any difficult question in natural philosophy, but shall be glad to have your opinion on a subject much more interesting.   What that is I will tell you.   In perusing a magazine some time ago I met with an account of a person who had been drowned.   He had continued under water 24 hours, and upon being properly treated when taken out he was restored to life.   The fact is undoubted, and upon enquiry I have found that there have been many instances of the same kind.   Physicians say that when the parts of the body are restrained from performing their functions by any gentle cause which does not in any manner maim or injure any particular part, that to restore life in such a case nothing is requisite but to give the vital warmth to the whole body by gentle degrees, and to put the blood in motion by inflating the lungs.   But the doubts which arose in my mind on reading the story were of another nature.   We are generally taught that the soul leaves the body at the instant of death, that is, at the instant in which the organs of the body cease to perform their functions, but does not this story contradict this opinion?   When then does the soul take its departure?   Let me have your opinion candidly and at length on this subject, and as these are doubts which, were they to come to light, might do injustice to a man's moral principles in the eyes of persons of narrow and confined views it will be proper to take great care of our letters. I propose as one means of doing it to put no name or place to the top or bottom of the letter, and to inclose it in a false cover which may be burned as soon as opened.   No news in town only that Sir John Cockler has given Knox 450 for his house and lots here. Orion is 3 Hours and 40′ west of the sun and of consequence goes down and rises that much before him, so you must rise early to see him. The upper star in his belt is exactly in the Equinoctial.

The two other letters in Mr. Wilkie's collection I also quote because one illustrates Jefferson's courtly politeness and the other his insatiable interest in economics and sociology. Both were written when Jefferson was living in Paris as United States Minister to France. The allusion in the second letter to what is now Pittsburgh and to the Ohio River foreshadows his imperial work in the Lewis and Clark expedition and the Louisiana Purchase.

DEAR SIR: Paris, May 29, 1786.
This will be handed you by Mr. Paradise who married a daughter of the late Col. Ludwell of Virginia, and who now comes to that country to make preparations for establishing himself and family in it. As a stranger and man of character he would have all the benefit of your civilities and attentions: but as a man of letters, of the purest integrity, of perfect goodness and republican simplicity, you will consider his acquaintance and friendship as a valuable acquisition. In confidence that by making you acquainted I serve and gratify both, I commit him to your friendly regards, with assurances of the esteem with which I have the honour to be Dear Sir.

Your friend and servt.
TH. JEFFERSON.

J. PAGE, ESQ.

Paris
May 4, 1786.

DEAR SIR:

Your two favours of Mar. 15 and Aug. 23, 1785 by
Monsieur de la Croix came to hand on the 15th of Novem-
ber.   His return gives me an opportunity of sending you a
copy of the Nautical Almanacs for 1786, 7, 8, 9.   There
is no late and interesting publication here or I would send
it by the same conveiance.   . . .

I thank you much for your communications.   Nothing
can be more grateful at such a distance.   It is unfortunate
that most people think the occurrences passing daily under
their eyes, are either known to all the world or not worth
being known.   They therefore do not give them place
in their letters.   I hope you will be so good as to continue
your friendly information.   The proceedings of our public
bodies, the progress of the public mind in interesting
questions, the casualties which happen among our private
friends, and whatever is interesting to yourself and family
will always be anxiously received by me.   There is one
circumstance in the work you were concerned in which has
not yet come to my knowledge, to wit: How far westward
from Fort Pitt does the Western Boundary of Pennsyl-
vania pass, and where does it strike the Ohio?   . . .

I returned but three or four days ago from a two months
trip to England.   I traversed that country much, and own
both town and country fell short of my expectations.
Comparing it with this I found a much greater proportion
of barrens, a soil in other parts not naturally so good as
this, not better cultivated, but better manured and therefore more productive.   This proceeds from the practice
of long leases there, and short ones here.   The labouring
people here are poorer than in England.   They pay about
one half their produce in rent, the English in general about
a third.   The gardening in that country is the article in

which it surpasses all the earth. I mean their pleasure gardening. This indeed went far beyond my ideas. The City of London, tho' handsomer than Paris, is not so handsome as Philadelphia. Their architecture is in the most wretched stile I ever saw, not meaning to except America where it is bad, nor even Virginia where it is worse than in any other part of America which I have seen. The mechanical arts in London are carried to a wonderful perfection, but of these I need not speak, because of them my countrymen have unfortunately too many samples before their eyes. I consider the extravagance which has seized them as a more baneful evil than toryism was during the war. It is the more so as the example is set by the best and most amiable characters among us. Would a missionary appear who would make frugality the basis of his religious system, and go thro the land preaching it up as the only road to salvation, I would join his school tho' not generally disposed to seek my religion out of the dictates of my own reason and feelings of my own heart. These things have been more deeply impressed on my mind by what I have heard and seen in England. That nation hates us, their ministers hate us, and their King more than all other men. They have the impudence to avow this, though they acknowledge our trade important to them, but they say we cannot prevent our countrymen from bringing that into their laps. A conviction of this determines them to make no terms of commerce with us. They say they will pocket our carrying trade as well as their own. Our overtures of commercial arrangement have been treated with derision which shew their firm persuasion that we shall never unite to suppress their commerce or even to impede it. I think their hostility towards us is much more deeply rooted at present than during the war. In the arts the most striking thing I saw there, new, was the application of the principle

of the steam-engine to grist mills. I saw 8 pr. of stones which are worked by steam, and they are to set up 30 pair in the same house. A hundred bushels of coal a day are consumed at present. I do not know in what proportion the consumption will be increased by the additional geer. . . .

Your affectionate friend & servt,
TH. JEFFERSON.

Jefferson's library of nearly seven thousand volumes at Monticello was the finest in the country, and, when, in his last years, through a too generous hospitality on a too meagre income, he fell into financial straits, it was parsimoniously bought and parsimoniously cared for by Congress. Some of the library was destroyed by fire in 1851, but the books that were saved may still be seen, carefully preserved in the Library of Congress. Among these books are volumes in Greek, Latin, French, Italian, Spanish, German, Norse, Gaelic, and Hebrew. One of the bonds which tie Jefferson to the group selected for the essays of the present volume is that he owned and read some of the works of Erasmus. Jefferson kept up his habits of reading to the end of his life. A great granddaughter describes them:

On winter evenings, when it grew too dark to read, in the half hour which passed before the candles came in, as we all sat round the fire, he taught us several childish games, and would play them with us. I remember that "Cross

questions," and "I love my love with an A." were two I
learned from him; and we would teach some of ours to him.
When the candles were brought, all was quiet immediately,
for he took up his book to read; and we would not speak out
of a whisper, lest we should disturb him; and generally
we followed his example and took a book; and I have seen
him raise his eyes from his own book, and look round on
the little circle of readers and smile, and make some remark to mamma about it.

It was Jefferson's love of letters that led him
to take so deep an interest in education and to
found the University of Virginia.

His ideas of the scope of public education [says Merwin]
went far beyond those which prevailed in his time, and
considerably beyond those which prevail even now. For
example, a free university course for the most apt pupils
graduated at the grammar schools, made part of his
scheme—an idea most nearly realized in the Western
States.

To Jefferson style was something more than a
mere embellishment of literature. Although a
lawyer, he found it hard to tolerate the involu-
tions of legal phraseology. In 1815, in preparing
by request a bill to establish public education in
Virginia, he wrote to a friend, a member of the
Virginia Legislature:

I dislike the verbose and intricate style of the modern
English statutes, and in our revised code I endeavoured to
restore it to the simple one of the ancient statutes in such

original bills as I drew in that work. I suppose the reformation has not been acceptable, as it has been little followed. You however can easily correct this bill to the taste of my brother lawyers, by making every other word a "said" or "aforesaid," and saying everything over two or three times, so as that nobody but we of the craft can untwist the diction and find out what it means.

The result of Jefferson's activity in behalf of public education was the founding of the University of Virginia. It is literally his creation, physically and intellectually. For five years he personally supervised the planning and construction of its beautiful campus and buildings; his achievements prove that he was one of the first of American architects—first not only in point of time, but in ability and creative genius. Although sixty-six years of age when the work began, he rode back and forth from Monticello almost daily in the saddle, a round journey of ten miles. But this is not surprising, for he was known throughout the countryside as a judge of blooded horses and a first-rate equestrian. In these days at West Point he would be able to take high rank in hippology. He was the first to establish the so-called elective system in university education, for he proposed to allow his students "uncontrolled choice in the lectures they shall choose to attend." To this freedom of choice there was one exception. Jefferson believed that the most technical scientist must have a sound knowledge of literature; and so, two years before his death, he wrote in his official capacity as Rector, the following in the Minutes of the University:

> No diploma shall be given to anyone who has not passed such an examination of the Latin language as shall have proved him able to read the highest classics in that language with ease, thorough understanding, and just quantity; and if he be also a proficient in the Greek let that too be stated in his diploma; the intention being that the reputation of the University shall not be committed but to those who, to an eminence in some one or more of the sciences taught in it, add a proficiency in these languages which constitute the basis of good education and are indispensable to fill up the character of a "well-educated man."

Jefferson's personal characteristics have been variously estimated by friends and foes. He was tall, ungainly, loose-jointed, and red-headed. That he was tolerant and kindly is unquestionable, but he was hated by his political antagonists, although adored by his followers and beloved by his family and his servants. When Philadelphia was the capital of the young nation, Jefferson, notwithstanding his rank as Vice President, was ostracized by the Federalists, who then controlled what passed for aristocratic

society. They despised him for a demagogue
and feared him as a radical. But when he was
elected President, even Gouverneur Morris, who
disliked and distrusted him, paid a tribute, on behalf of the Senate, to the "intelligence, attention,
and impartiality" with which Jefferson had pre-
sided over the deliberations of that body. This
means something, for Morris, in his diary, reports
with satisfaction that Madame de Flahaut, a
notorious but influential leader in Parisian society,
had said to him, after first "seeing Jefferson's
countenance" when he was Minister to France,
"*Cet homme est faux et emport*"—an untrust-
worthy and headstrong man. But as Madame
de Flahaut, married at fifteen to an aristocratic
roué, fell in love with the tutor employed by her
husband to give her an education—the Abbé
Périgord, who became the father of her only
child—her moral judgments may be taken with
some reservation. Her estimate of Jefferson,
however, is confirmed by one of his most enthusiastic eulogists, Claude G. Bowers, who admits
that

there is one unpleasant criticism of his manner that cannot
be so easily put aside—a shiftiness in his glance which
bears out the charge of his enemies that he was lacking in
frankness. The most democratic member of the first

Senate, meeting him for the first time, was disappointed to find that "he had a rambling vacant look, and nothing of that firm collected deportment which I expected would dignify the presence of a Secretary or Minister." Another found that "when speaking he did not look at his auditor, but cast his eyes toward the ceiling or anywhere but at the eye of his auditor." This weakness was possibly over-emphasized, for he was notoriously shy.

Later, when Jefferson was President, Morris said of him:

He believes in the perfectibility of man, the wisdom of mobs, and the moderation of Jacobins. He believes in the payment of debts by diminution of revenue, in defense of territory by reduction of armies, and in vindication of rights by appointment of ambassadors.

But this is the opinion of an ardent Hamiltonian.

That Jefferson had a charm of character which overrode political prejudices is shown by his relation to the Adamses. In 1786, when John Adams was Minister to England and Jefferson was Minister to France they lived, both in London and Paris, on terms of affectionate intimacy. Abigail Adams, whose standards of conduct and character were as rigid as those of a Biblical prophet, was a devoted admirer of Jefferson and wrote home that he was one of the "chosen of the earth." But on the succession of Adams to the Presidency the friendship cooled. Jefferson suspected Adams of monarchical leanings; Adams appointed Marshall as Chief Justice partly to forestall what he regarded as Jefferson's loose and dangerous democratic tendencies. The friendship which had thus been broken in middle life by violent antagonisms was renewed, however, in their old age, and they found mutual solace in a correspondence that is noteworthy in epistolary literature. The attachment of the stern old New England Puritan for the polished Virginian Liberal is revealed by the last words which Adams is reported to have uttered on his deathbed—"Thomas Jefferson still lives!"

The judgment of a man's servants is not a bad index to his character. Jefferson was beloved by his. Hirst tells the story of the loyalty of his slaves when he was driven from Monticello during the Revolution by Captain McLeod of Tarleton's dragoons, escaping capture by a hair's-breadth:

Two faithful slaves, Martin and Cæsar, were depositing plate and valuables under the planked floor of the front portico. Martin was above, Cæsar in the dark hole below. Seeing the troopers, Martin dropped the plank and left Cæsar below where he remained undiscovered and without food for the next eighteen hours. Martin, as master of ceremonies, received the unwelcome visitors and showed the Captain through the house, just as a mediæval seneschal might have led some robber chieftain over a surrendered castle. When they came to the study, McLeod looked round for a few minutes, then locked the door and gave the key to Martin. The soldiers took some wine from the cellar, but otherwise nothing was touched or injured. Tarleton, it seems, had left strict orders to that effect. This story of the British soldiers' visit to Monticello was the delight of Jefferson's children and grandchildren, who often heard it from him and from Cæsar. Martin died soon afterwards; but Cæsar, a great favourite, lived to a good old age.

Again when Jefferson returned to Monticello, after his long absence in France as Minister Plenipotentiary, his slaves displayed their devotion to him. Jefferson's daughter Martha, who went with him to France and accompanied him home, thus describes the scene:

There were no stages in those days. We were indebted to the kindness of our friends for horses; and visiting all the way homeward, and spending more or less time with them all in turn, we reached Monticello on the 23rd of December. The Negroes discovered the approach of the carriage as soon as it reached Shadwell, and such a scene I never witnessed in my life. They collected in crowds around it, and almost drew it up the mountain by hand. When the door of the carriage was open, they received him in their arms and bore him to the house, crowding around and kissing his hands and feet—some blubbering and crying—others laughing.

Martha's education in France, it may be said in passing, under the supervision of her father, is a tribute both to his paternal affection and to his gifts as a teacher. He constantly encouraged her in her studies, laying stress upon style and a knowledge of literature, with what success is indicated by the vivid simplicity with which she relates the foregoing anecdote.

Jefferson spent his old age in peace and happiness at Monticello, the beautiful home which he had created for his bride nearly fifty years before, the bride whose memory he always cherished although she preceded him to the grave by more than forty years. His chief occupation in the last years of his life was the building of the University of Virginia; but such leisure hours as that left him he spent in a varied correspondence, in counselling the members of his party who turned to him as their recognized political sage, in gardening, and in tranquil domestic pleasures with his children and grandchildren. At his death his body was buried in the ground at Monticello, which he loved so well, and in accordance with his written request there stands above the grave a simple stone monument on which may be read to-day the following inscription but, in obedience to his specific direction, "not a word more."

Here was buried
Thomas Jefferson
Author of the Declaration of American Independence,
Of the Statute of Virginia for Religious Freedom,
And Father of the University of Virginia.

Whatever may be one's feelings about the fallacy of some of Jefferson's political philosophy and the inconsistencies of his statesmanship, they fade away as one stands at Monticello before this modest monument and reads its simple but noble record of a spiritual and intellectual aristocrat.

JOHN MARSHALL

THE DEMOCRAT

THE DEMOCRAT
BORN 1755—DIED 1835

ONE of the many amusing stories told of Dr. Jowett, the Master of Balliol College, Oxford, the famous translator of Plato, is apropos. One evening, at his dinner table, his guests, among whom were two or three fellow clergymen of the Church of England and two or three members of the English bar, fell into a discussion as to which is the more honourable and distinguished office, that of a judge or that of a bishop. The lawyers claimed that a judge is more powerful, because he can say, "You be hanged." The clergymen asserted that a bishop exercises greater authority because he can say, "You be damned." "Yes," commented Jowett with the gentle irony that was his characteristic, "but when a judge says 'You be hanged' you *are* hanged."

This story throws some light on the reason why Marshall's name is less familiar to his countrymen than those of half a dozen founders of the Republic among whom he deserves to rank on equal terms. It is true that he is generally thought of as a great judge. But there is nothing romantic in the popular conception of great judges. They command respect but not affection. They have no political following. They do not perform deeds of physical valour. They do not stir the emotions with eloquence. They appeal to the intellect rather than to the imagination.

It is a trite thing to say that the Constitution is the foundation stone of our republic. If it should ever cease to be revered and obeyed by a majority of American citizens, the republic would fall in ruins. It is conceivable, of course, that some other form of government, some other phase of national life, might rise to take its place, but it would not be the United States of America as conceived by our fathers. I do not know where to find, not even in James Bryce's monumental work, *The American Commonwealth*, a better description of the Constitutional Convention than the following from an unknown writer in the *International Encyclopædia:*

There nas been only one National Constitutional Convention in the United States—that which framed the Constitution; but the high character of this assemblage, the patriotic spirit and wisdom which animated it, and

the astonishing success which has attended its labours,
have made it the immortal type of such gatherings. In
the United States its members are revered as the "Fathers
of the Constitution."

They should certainly be so revered. But
Marshall, although not a member of the Convention, deserves equal reverence with the
Fathers who framed the Constitution, for it was
he who made of the splendid document a living
and continuing thing. In some respects we owe
more to him than to any other of the Founders.
Washington gave the United States liberty;
Marshall gave them permanency. If it had not
been for him it is not improbable that the greatest united democracy that civilization has ever
known might have been a mere collection of
feeble, antagonistic, and warring republics. It
was Marshall who laid down the principles by
which Lincoln led the country out of secession
into union. It may even be said that, if Marshall had not lived, Germany might have been
the victor in the World War. For if that portion
of North America which is now the United States
had been a congeries of little nations—a New
England republic, a Central Atlantic republic, a
South Atlantic republic, a Mississippi republic,
a Pacific republic, a Northwestern republic—no
United States army and navy could have struck

the final blow that put an end to Prussian despotism. These are broad and may, perhaps, seem extravagant statements to make about any American, especially about one in whose life, character, and place in history the general public has, comparatively, shown so little interest. Are such tributes to Marshall's greatness mere rhetorical flourishes or can they be substantiated? I believe they are substantial and that his profound and intimate influence on current life warrant his inclusion among the great modernists.

Marshall was the fourth Chief Justice of the Supreme Court of the United States—fourth in the order of service but, in the order of achievements and influence, first and greatest of the ten who have held that exalted office. While not its founder, he may be said to have been the creator of the court. He was preceded in his office by John Jay of New York, John Rutledge of South Carolina, and Oliver Ellsworth of Connecticut. Under these predecessors, perhaps through no fault of their own, the Supreme Court was a feeble institution. Jay resigned his position because he was

perfectly convinced that under a system so defective it [the Supreme Court] would not obtain the energy, weight, and dignity which was essential to its affording due support to the national government; nor acquire the public confidence and respect, which, as a last resort of the justice of the nation, it should possess.

When Marshall, at the age of forty-six, was appointed by President Adams in 1801 to be Chief Justice, it was he who almost single handed gave it the authority, dignity, and confidence, the lack of which Jay deplored, and made it what it is to-day, the final arbiter of our national life.

Few men stop to think how the decisions of the Supreme Court are woven into their daily doings. It is the Supreme Court, not Congress, which imposed the income tax and established woman suffrage. It is the Supreme Court which decides whether or not we shall prohibit the saloon, abolish child labour, enact maternity and infant mortality laws, regulate sweatshops in tenements, apply tests to our milk supply in order to prevent tuberculosis. The Supreme Court has the power to tell us how we shall educate our children, clean our streets, rent our houses and apartments, and whether the railroads shall mine our coal and how they shall transport it. By the exercise of learning and wisdom, and by devotion to duty and unquestioned patriotism for a hundred years, the Supreme Court has acquired such dignity and moral power that the country willingly submits to its authority. The reason why this country with its enormous area and population, with its conflicting and sectional interests, has not been frequently torn by rebellion and revolution, is because its citizens have been educated to respect and abide by the Court's decisions. The history of the present income-tax law is a striking example of the submission of the people to the decisions of the Court.

In 1894, responding to manifest public opinion, Congress passed an income-tax law. The machinery was set in motion for the collection of the tax. I remember making a return of my income to the revenue agent of my district at the time. But the constitutionality of the law was attacked upon the ground that it was a violation of the article of the Constitution which provides that direct taxes shall be apportioned among the several states according to their population. The Supreme Court sustained this protest by a five-to-four vote, and even this close decision was made after one of the judges had changed his opinion. If there ever was a case for resentment against the Supreme Court for incompetency here it was. But the country accepted the authority of the Court and proceeded by the slow process of amendment to cure the defect in the law. This took nearly twenty years.

The point is that the people finally obtained
their object, not by outcry or rebellion, but by
orderly procedure under the direction of the
Court. It was John Marshall who gave this
basic institution its supreme authority. Before
considering his personality, it is desirable to
consider how he accomplished this unprecedented
achievement.

In 1801, when Jefferson assumed the Presidency and Marshall the Chief Justiceship, these
two great Virginians were the acknowledged
champions of two fundamental and opposing
ideas of the philosophy and structure of our
government. John Marshall believed in a strong
and sovereign nation. His military and political
experiences in the Revolution were such that he
was, as he himself once said, "confirmed in the
habit of considering America as my country and
Congress as my government." Thomas Jefferson believed in the sovereignty of the several
states which he contended had associated themselves in a confederacy without surrendering
their sovereign powers. It is not surprising that
Marshall and Jefferson came into conflict or that
Jefferson bitterly opposed Marshall and the
growing authority of the Supreme Court under
Marshall's leadership. The conflict came to a
culmination in the famous case of Marbury

versus Madison. It was in this case that Marshall laid down the principle that the Supreme Court may declare a law of Congress (and, by implication, of a State Legislature) to be unconstitutional and therefore null and void. William Marbury, an insignificant person except for his connection with this historic case, had been appointed Justice of the Peace in the District of Columbia by President Adams on the eve of the latter's retirement from office. When Jefferson was inaugurated, he ordered his Secretary of State, Madison, not to deliver the commission to Marbury, whereupon Marbury applied to the Supreme Court for a mandamus, or an order from the Court, commanding the President and his Secretary of State to give Marbury his commission. Marshall, by a stroke of genius, while asserting Jefferson's injustice to Marbury, decreed that the law under which the latter sought redress was unconstitutional, thus killing two birds with one stone—the two birds being the attempts of Jefferson, on the one hand, to cripple the political party to which Marshall belonged, and, on the other, to establish the supremacy of the executive over the judicial branch of the government. The Marbury decision once and for all made the Supreme Court really supreme. As I am writing for laymen and not for lawyers, it will not, I hope, be considered impertinent if I attempt to condense and paraphrase Marshall's reasoning as follows:

Marbury was legally appointed and could not legally under the Constitution be removed or restrained from office except for malfeasance. A President cannot be interfered with by the courts in making an appointment but, the appointment once having been made and confirmed, the appointee has a vested right which he can defend in the courts even against the President. If a purchaser of public lands is granted by the constitutional authority a patent to those lands and the Secretary of State withholds the patent, the purchaser has a legal remedy for the injustice which he suffers.

The withholding of Marbury's commission was a plain violation of his constitutional vested right. Is a mandamus the proper remedy? It is. But what court shall issue the writ? Can the Supreme Court do so? Section 13 of the Judiciary Law of 1789 says that the Supreme Court shall issue such writs. If the Supreme Court cannot issue such a writ it must be because the Judiciary Law of 1789 is a violation of the Constitution. The Constitution defines exactly in what kinds of cases the Supreme Court shall have original jurisdiction and says that in all other cases its jurisdiction shall be appellate. Mandamus proceedings are not included among the cases defined by the Constitution for original jurisdiction. But the law of 1789 says that the Supreme Court may originate a writ of mandamus. The Constitution says it may not. Which shall the Court obey, the Constitution or the Congress? If it obeys the Congress the Constitution is not worth the paper it is written on and our nation will fall to pieces, for its very existence depends on the Constitution. That fundamental document cannot be changed or amended by Congress alone. The process of amendment is defined by the Constitution itself. When the Court is confronted with a law which plainly contradicts the Constitution it must declare that law null and void.

Marbury was duly appointed Justice of the Peace; the withholding of his commission is an injustice; he has a legal remedy; that legal remedy is a mandamus; but the law under which he asks the Supreme Court to issue the writ, not on appeal from a lower court but in original jurisdiction, is unconstitutional. His plea is denied.

Such was the apparent ease with which Marshall stated a principle that has made and saved a great nation. But the ease should not surprise us; the outstanding quality of genius is the appearance of ease with which it performs unprecedented feats.

The United States has been carved out of frontier country. It is therefore quite in the nature of things that many of her leaders have been of the pioneer type. Washington, although an aristocrat by birth and breeding, was an accomplished woodsman; Lincoln was a backwoodsman; even Roosevelt had a pioneer spirit. Marshall came from a family of pioneers. He was born, the son of a pioneer, in the backwoods on the frontier of Virginia. His father was of humble artisan origin. His mother, Senator Beveridge tells us, although her ancestry was of the English gentry, "like most other women of that region and period, seldom had such things as pins; in place of them use was made of thorns plucked from the bushes in the woods." Although plain people these parents were sterling in character and were looked up to as leaders in their circle. The father was a friend of Washington and was employed by Washington on surveying parties. Schools were few and far between, and Marshall's early education was obtained at home. He had, of course, access to few books, but those that he read were good. Pope's poems were a part of his favourite boyhood reading. That his taste in literature was judicious is shown by a letter which he wrote when Chief Justice, to Story, his devoted friend and associate. Story had delivered a Phi Beta Kappa oration at Harvard and had failed to mention Jane Austen in the list of authors whom he memorialized. In commenting on the oration Marshall wrote:

I was a little mortified to find that you had not admitted the name of Miss Austen into your list of favourites. I had just finished reading her novels when I received your discourse and was so much pleased with them that I looked in it for her name, and was rather disappointed at not finding it. Her flights are not lofty, she does not soar on eagle's wings, but she is pleasing, interesting, equable, and yet amusing. I count on your making some apology for this omission.

Rudyard Kipling, who in *Debits and Credits*, has become the most recent champion of Jane Austen, could scarcely do better than this!

While living under conditions that from the modern point of view would be considered unpromising and even stunting, Marshall's boyhood and youth passed smoothly and happily. His father prospered, became sheriff, was elected a member of the Virginia House of Burgesses, and faithfully fulfilled the obligations of paternity to fifteen children of whom John, born in 1755, was the eldest. At twenty years of age the embryo Chief Justice became a lieutenant in a company of Revolutionary soldiers from Virginia. He was a leader both in his military duties and in athletics. He could run faster and jump higher than any of his comrades, and was known because of his speed as a runner and his agility in jumping as "Silver Heels." He served in the Revolutionary War with credit and was closely associated with Washington at Valley Forge. Here were first manifested those qualities of good temper and human understanding which later so marked his career as a lawyer and a judge. One of his fellow officers in Washington's army said of him:

He was the best tempered man I ever knew. During his sufferings at Valley Forge nothing discouraged, nothing disturbed him. If he had only bread to eat, it was just as well; if only meat, it made no difference; if any of the officers murmured at their deprivations, he would shame them by good-natured raillery or encourage them by his own exuberance of spirits. He was an excellent companion, and idolized by the soldiers and his brother officers, whose gloomy hours were enlivened by his inexhaustible fund of anecdotes:

This democratic affability was not repressed, but on the contrary developed and mellowed, by the honours and offices which came to him unsought as his career progressed. Senator Beveridge paints an engaging portrait of him when he became one of the leaders of the Richmond bar, a group of lawyers still remembered in legal annals for their attainments and abilities:

On a pleasant summer morning when the cherries were ripe, a tall, ungainly man in early middle life sauntered along a Richmond street. His long legs were encased in knee breeches, stockings and shoes of the period; and about his gaunt, bony frame hung a round-about or short linen jacket. Plainly, he had paid little attention to his attire. He was bareheaded and his unkempt hair was tied behind in a queue. He carried his hat under his arm, and it was full of cherries which the owner was eating as he sauntered idly along. Mr. Epp's hotel [the Eagle] faced the street along which this negligently apparelled person was making his leisurely way. He greeted the landlord as he approached, cracked a joke in passing, and rambled on in his unhurried walk.

At the inn was an old gentleman from the country who had come to Richmond where a lawsuit, to which he was party, was to be tried. The venerable litigant had a hundred dollars to pay to the lawyer who should conduct the case, a very large fee for those days. Who was the best lawyer in Richmond, asked he of his host? "The man who just passed us, John Marshall by name," said the tavernkeeper. But the countryman would have none of Marshall. His appearance did not fill the old man's idea of a practitioner before the courts. He wanted, for his hundred dollars, a lawyer who looked like a lawyer. He would go to the courtroom itself and there ask for further recommendation. But again he was told by the clerk of the court to retain Marshall, who, meanwhile, had ambled into the courtroom.

But no! This searcher for a legal champion would use his own judgment. Soon a venerable, dignified person, solemn of face, with black coat and powdered wig, entered the room. At once the planter retained him. The client remained in the courtroom, it appears, to listen to the lawyers in the other cases that were ahead of his own. Thus he heard the pompous advocate whom he had chosen; and then, in astonishment, listened to Marshall.

The attorney of impressive appearance turned out to be so inferior to the eccentric-looking advocate that the planter went to Marshall, frankly told him the circumstances, and apologized. Explaining that he had but five dollars left, the troubled old farmer asked Marshall whether he would conduct his case for that amount. With a kindly jest about the power of a black coat and powdered wig, Marshall good-naturedly accepted.

Even when he became Chief Justice, holding an office second only to that of the President in dignity and power, Marshall retained his

enjoyment of the simplest kind of social pleasures
as Senator Beveridge tells us:

When in Richmond the one sport in which he delighted
was the pitching of quoits. Not when a lawyer was he
a more enthusiastic or regular attendant of the meetings
of the Quoit Club, or Barbecue Club, under the trees at
Buchanan's Spring on the outskirts of Richmond, than
he was when at the height of his fame as Chief Justice of
the United States. More personal descriptions of Marshall at these gatherings have come down to us than exist
for any other phase of his life. Chester Harding, the
artist, when painting Marshall's portrait during the summer of 1826, spent some time in the Virginia Capital, and
attended one of the meetings of the Quoit Club. It was
a warm day, and presently Marshall, then in his seventy-
second year, was seen coming, his coat on his arm, fanning
himself with his hat. Walking straight up to a bowl
of mint julep, he poured a tumbler full of the liquid, drank
it off, said, "How are you, gentlemen?" and fell to pitching
quoits with immense enthusiasm. When he won, says
Harding, "the woods would ring with his triumphant
shout."

James K. Paulding went to Richmond for the purpose
of talking to the Chief Justice and observing his daily life.
He was more impressed by Marshall's gaiety and un-
restraint at the Quoit Club than by anything else he
noted. "The Chief Justice threw off his coat," relates
Paulding, "and fell to work with as much energy as he
would have directed to the decision of . . . the
conflicting jurisdiction of the General and the State governments." During the game a dispute arose between
two players "as to the quoit nearest the peg." Marshall
was agreed upon as umpire. "The judge bent down on
one knee and with a straw essayed the decision of this

important question . . . frequently biting off the end of the straw" for greater accuracy.

It must not be inferred from these simple pleasures that Marshall had a simple mind. It was so profound and so original, on the contrary, that it amounted to genius. What genius is or what its source no one has yet succeeded in defining, although there have been many epigrammatic descriptions of it. It is certainly not an original product of education. Marshall had as little formal education as Keats. His schooling was rudimentary. It is true that he attended a few law lectures by George Wythe, one of the signers of the Declaration of Independence and the best Latin and Greek scholar of the colonies, at William and Mary College, but his reading of law could not have been very deep or very wide. At that moment love interested him more than law books, and he left college to marry the charming daughter of a prominent Virginia family, settled in Richmond, and was admitted to the bar.

The first political office which Marshall held was that of membership in the Virginia Legislature. His character and ability made him a power in every good movement and a supporter of every wise enactment of law. The great question before the American people at that time was whether the Constitution should be ratified and a nation created out of the loose federation of colonies and states. The fate of the country trembled in the balance. Marshall at thirty-two was the leader of the Nationalists in the Virginia Constitutional Convention, and by his quiet, calm, and persuasive reasoning carried a majority with him. Virginia, intellectually and politically the most powerful of the states which then composed the Union, ratified the Constitution. If Virginia had rejected it the course of our history would have been changed. Marshall saved her from the calamity of rejection.

At the end of his second Presidency, Washington offered Marshall successively the Attorney Generalship and the position of Minister to France. Marshall declined both offers, preferring to retain his leadership at the bar, but in 1797 he went to France as one of the three special commissioners appointed by President Adams. The wisdom he displayed in this special mission resulted in his election to Congress. From Congress he was selected by President Adams as Secretary of State and from that office was appointed to the Chief Justiceship. On the bench as Chief Justice his opinions and decrees are models of precision, directness, and persuasiveness. Professor George W. Kirchwey, a distinguished jurisconsult, says of Marshall:

For thirty-four years he dominated the Court by his great learning, his masterful power of analysis and clearness of statement. Perhaps no judge ever excelled him in the capacity to hold a legal proposition before the eyes of others in such various forms and colours.

To a layman who reads Marshall's Constitutional decisions, as I frequently do for the beauty of their reasoning and the clearness of their style, one of their outstanding features is their freedom from disputatiousness. In his autobiography Benjamin Franklin deplores disputatiousness as

a very bad habit, making people often extremely disagreeable in company by the contradiction that is necessary to Lring it into practice; and thence, besides souring and spoiling the conversation, is productive of disgusts and, perhaps, enmities where you may have occasion for friendship. I had caught it by reading my father's books of disputes about religion. Persons of good sense, I have since observed, seldom fall into it, except lawyers, university men, and men of all sorts that have been bred at Edinborough.

Abraham Lincoln and John Marshall were lawyers who never fell into the error which Franklin thought was characteristic of members of the legal profession. The greatest of American Presidents and the greatest of American judges are shining exemplars of the power of kindly and tolerant persuasiveness.

The secret of Marshall's persuasiveness lies in the fact that while he was fearless he was never combative. While he was argumentative, he was never disputatious. The reasoning of his judicial decisions is so clear and direct, so Euclidian in its convincing simplicity, so free from technical and professional jargon, that they carry all before them. His method of argument was not that of a Mosaic lawgiver. He never said "Thou shalt" or "Thou shalt not," but, like Socrates, he led the minds of his hearers along until it seemed to them that they were pronouncing the judgment themselves. His method and sometimes his very language was this: "If such and such are the facts, and the evidence appears to me to establish them beyond a reasonable doubt, would not so and so be the logical deduction from those facts?" And then he would render a decision that appeared so inevitable and natural that even the contending lawyers in the courtroom would unconsciously nod their heads in assent, hardly realizing the deep philosophy and far-reaching consequences of the pronouncement.

Marshall was an affectionate father and devoted husband. In his domestic relations he displayed a quality which all men who are truly great possess, courtesy and chivalry toward women. This quality was so marked in him that Senator Beveridge records that it "remains to this day a living tradition in Richmond." His courtship and marriage were tinged with a beautiful tenderness for his wife who was long an invalid. "By Marshall's direction," says Senator Beveridge, "the last thing taken from his body after he expired was the locket which his wife had hung about his neck just before she died." The day after his funeral in Richmond on July 9, 1835, the Richmond *Whig and Public Advertiser* expressed the general feeling when it said: "No man has lived or died in this country, save its father George Washington alone, who united such a warmth of affection for his person with so deep and so unaffected a respect for his character and admiration for his great ability."

Such was the soldier, the statesman, the administrator of justice, the citizen whose name should be remembered with pride and admiration not only as an American patriot but as one of the great founders, together with Littleton, Blackstone, and Mansfield, of modern law. Moreover, he was one of the great champions of democracy. For without the just arbitrament of law there can be no such thing as democratic rights or economic freedom.

BEETHOVEN

THE POET

SEVEN:

THE POET

BORN 1770—DIED 1827

THE story of Beethoven is the most depressing of the twelve I have undertaken to tell. Only the splendour of his creative genius relieves the narrative from the mists of disappointment and despondency with which it is darkened. But against this sombre background his innate nobility of spirit shines all the more clearly.

Ludwig van Beethoven was born in Bonn in 1770, many years before that city became famous as the seat of one of the great German universities. The family was a Dutch or Flemish one, which explains the "van" in the composer's name. Beethoven's ancestors were of humble origin. His grandfather was an inconspicuous professional singer in Louvain and emigrated to Bonn where he earned a modest income as chief Court Musician of the petty prince or Elector of that city. He was forced to eke out this income by opening a wine shop or, as one of Beethoven's German biographers politely puts it, by carrying on the business of a vintner. This avocation explains, the same biographer thinks, the notorious drunkenness of the composer's grandmother and father. His grandmother had to be confined in an asylum toward the end of her life because of her inebriety and his father was barely rescued from a drunkard's death in the gutter. The grandfather, Louis van Beethoven, in spite of the degeneracy of his wife and son, appears to have been a man of character and probity, and Beethoven, throughout his life, looked back to him with "pride and reverence." Beethoven's mother was the daughter of the head cook in the local palace, and when she married his father was the widow of the valet of one of the minor rulers of the neighbourhood. But she was gentle and good and inspired her son with a real affection, although she seems to have had little influence in his education or upbringing.

Everything in Beethoven's boyhood might have been expected to disgust him with music, but the inexplicable, compelling force of creative genius cannot be thwarted. Another notable example of the operation of this indisputable law of life is found in the career of the French painter Jean François Millet. Like the needle to the pole star, Millet was drawn irresistibly to paper and pencil and canvas and colours. The most disconcerting obstacles could not divert him from his goal. In like manner, Beethoven was created for music, and nothing, neither poverty nor the paucity of education nor the harshness of his father nor deafness nor the misunderstanding and antagonism of contemporaries nor the bitterness of family life, could separate him from it.

Beethoven made his first public appearance when he was eight years of age at a concert organized by his father. On this occasion he played, so the published advertisement informs us, "various clavier concertos and trios." But he did not take up the serious study of the piano until a year later when his master, a travelling musician and a crony of his father's, gave him irregular lessons. This teacher was a skillful pianist but a hard taskmaster. "Often," says Thayer, "when he came with Beethoven, the father, from the wine house late at night, the boy was roused from sleep and kept at the piano-forte until morning." Ludwig was also trained in the use of other instruments. When still very young he played the second violin and the viola in the orchestra of the National Theatre of Bonn. It was this experience that, at an early age, gave him a familiarity with the intricacies of orchestral scoring and composition. He was also an accomplished organist, and played that instrument professionally and with skill when he was twelve years old. His best teacher of that noble instrument was a friar of the Order of St. Francis, who employed him to play the organ at the six o'clock morning mass at the Church of the Minorites in Bonn. Thus Beethoven is related, in a way, with another of the twelve modernists whose lives afford the material of the biographical sketches that compose the present volume.

Although he was a skilled organist and a successful orchestral player of the viola and the violin, the piano was really his instrument. In his boyhood days, the harpsichord or the piano was one of the regular instruments of a symphonic orchestra, and at twelve years of age Beethoven became "cembalist," or pianist, of the orchestra maintained by the Elector in Bonn. At this time he played the preludes and fugues of Bach and read difficult scores at sight in a way to excite universal admiration. Later on, when he was breaking into the musical circles of Vienna, the father of Czerny, the Austrian composer, met on the streets a popular pianist, long since forgotten, the Abbé Gelinek by name. Observing that the Abbé was dressed as if for some formal occasion, Czerny asked him where he was bound. "I am asked," was the reply, "to measure myself with a young pianist who has just arrived named Beethoven; I'll use him up." A few days later Czerny met the Abbé again. "Well, how was it?"—"Ah, he is no man; he's a devil. He will play me and all of us to death. And how he improvises!"

Gelinek was not the only one who thought there was something supernatural or abnormal about the genius of Beethoven. Thayer quotes the following reminiscence from William Gardiner, an Englishman, which shows not only that Beethoven had achieved the reputation of a composer at twenty-three years of age, but that his compositions were so modern as to be denounced as incomprehensible and as violations of all known and normal standards:

My company was sought with that of two of my friends to make up occasionally an instrumental quartett [the fourth member being a German exiled from Bonn, the Abbé Dobbeler]. . . . Our music consisted of the Quartetts of Haydn, Boccherini, and Wranizky. The Abbé, who never travelled without his violin, had luckily put into his fiddle case a Trio composed by Beethoven, just before he set off, which thus, in the year 1793, found its way to Leicester. This composition, so different from anything I had ever heard, awakened in me a new sense, a new delight in the science of sounds. . . . When I went to town [London] I enquired for the works of this author, but could learn nothing more than that he was considered a madman and that his music was like himself. However, I had a friend in Hamburg through whom, although the war was raging at the time, I occasionally obtained some of these inestimable treasures.

At twenty-two years of age Beethoven removed to Vienna, then the musical capital of Europe, and lived there for the rest of his somewhat stormy life. He intended to be a composer, although he was recognized as a piano virtuoso of the first rank and supported himself by giving lessons upon that instrument. He also studied composition, but soon found that he was himself the best master of the theory of music. Even the great Haydn, from whom he sought instruction, failed to satisfy his needs. In Vienna, too, he met with his first social repulse. He proposed to a famous singer and was refused on the ground that he was "too ugly." He was fond of the society of women, had high ideals with regard to them, and formed some beautiful and inspiring friendships with them. But, either because of his marked personal eccentricities, which sometimes gravitated into extreme disorderliness, or for some other unexplained reason, his not infrequent dreams of happy marriage came to naught, and he lavished his instinctive paternal love upon a worthless and ungrateful nephew and died as he lived, a solitary spirit. This, perhaps, is not surprising for

in his behaviour [says Ferdinand Ries, who was one of his pupils], Beethoven was awkward and helpless; his uncouth movements were often destitute of all grace. He seldom took anything into his hands without dropping and breaking it. Thus he frequently knocked his inkwell into the pianoforte, which stood near by the side of his writing table. No piece of furniture was safe from him, least of all a costly piece. Everything was overturned, soiled and destroyed. It is hard to comprehend how he accomplished so much as to be able to shave himself, even leaving out of consideration the number of cuts on his cheeks. He could never learn to dance in time. Beethoven attached no value to his manuscripts; after they were printed they lay for the greater part in an anteroom or on the floor among the other pieces of music. I often put his music to rights; but whenever he hunted something, everything was thrown into confusion again.

But these are only superficial peculiarities. In spite of them, the very man who recorded them adored Beethoven, who repaid his devotion with affectionate trust and reliance. Beethoven is not to be judged by externals but by a deeper standard which has been better interpreted by an anonymous writer in a recent issue of the London *Times* than by any other commentator that I have run across:

For many people Beethoven is . . . the greatest artist who ever lived. They do not say that his music is more beautiful than that of all other composers, but they do say that its spiritual content is more profound and more valuable. . . . His real life was an inner life, a life richer and more profound than any other artist has expressed; and, as if by design, he was given such characteristics as effectually protected him from the outer world and its influences. He had no conventions, social or other, he was impervious to criticism, and there was no social passion or emotion, not even sexual love, to which he could be permanently subjected. He was free to bend all his tremendous energies to the task of self-development. He lived in a world whose values were not his and the contrast made him sometimes angry and bewildered. As he grew older, his impatience and contempt sometimes made him also unscrupulous. But the great task he came to perform was never shirked. In him humanity reached a peak, prophetic of the future development of the race. To climb so high the soul must pass through great suffering and be brought to the verge of despair. Only an unflinching courage and indomitable will can enable a man to pay the price demanded. Beethoven's music is the proof that he paid the price to the uttermost farthing.

For thirty-five years Beethoven lived in Vienna, leaving it rarely. His external life was full of all sorts of irritations. "He had," says Paul Bekker, his latest and perhaps his most understanding biographer, "household worries, lawsuits, and domestic intrigues to contend with." These irritations aggravated his natural ill health. "Almost every year his health suffered from some fresh assault; he was attacked in turn by jaundice, rheumatism, an obstinate eye trouble, and peritonitis." But what the layman would naturally consider the most insurmountable obstacle to the work of a musician was his deafness. Symptoms of this infirmity began to show themselves when he was twenty years old. By the time he was thirty it became clear that the obscure aural disease was progressive and incurable. When it began Beethoven's first feeling was one of fear, then of despair, and then of a kind of resignation. He was supported, and even deterred from suicide, only by the realization of his creative gift and his determination to give it expression in composition. In 1801, twenty-six years before his death, he wrote to a friend:

I am stronger and better; only my ears whistle and buzz continually, day and night. I can only say I am living a wretched life; for two years I have avoided almost all social gatherings because it is impossible for me to say to people: "I am deaf." If I belonged to any other profession it would be easier, but in my profession it is an awful state, the more since my enemies, who are not few, what would they say? In order to give you an idea of this singular deafness of mine I must tell you that in the theatre I must get very close to the orchestra in order to understand the actor. If I am a little distant I do not hear the high tones of the instruments, singers, and if I be but a little farther away I do not hear at all. Frequently I can hear the tones of a low conversation, but not the words, and as soon as anybody shouts it is intolerable. . . . I have often cursed my existence; Plutarch taught me resignation. If possible I will bid defiance to my fate, although there will be moments in my life when I shall be the unhappiest of God's creatures.

And yet, six years after this letter was written, he composed his immortal Fifth Symphony. In 1824, at the first performance of his Ninth, or Choral, Symphony, when he appeared on the stage as the composer he had to be turned around by a woman singer of the chorus so that he could see the applause of the audience, which he could not hear. In a document which is known as the Heiligenstadt Will, but which is really a kind of rhapsody of the inmost feelings of Beethoven's soul, of the struggle there between black despair and heroic determination, the composer begs those who think him "malevolent, stubborn, or misanthropic" to remember his intolerable affliction in the loss of "the one sense which should have been more perfect in me than in others, a sense which I once possessed in the highest perfection, a perfection such as few surely in my profession enjoy or ever have enjoyed"; he records his determination to cultivate patience which he hopes "will remain firm to endure until it pleases the inexorable Parcæ to break the thread"; and he utters this pathetic prayer:

Divine One, thou lookest into my inmost soul, thou knowest it, thou knowest that love of man and desire to do good live therein. O men, when some day ye read these words, reflect that ye did me wrong and let the unfortunate one comfort himself and find one of his kind who, despite all the obstacles of nature, yet did all that was in power to be accepted among worthy artists and men.

Milton's blindness and Pasteur's paralysis are not comparable as cala mities and obstacles in the life of a man of genius with the deafness of Beethoven. It was a feature of his career that cannot be overem phasized, for it not only explains many of the brusque and repellent traits of his personality, bu t is an illustration, almost unparalleled in the range of biography, of the truth of Henley's poem which asserts that man is master of his fate.

To this great loa d borne by Beethoven was added the burden of financial perplexities and family disappointments. There is, or was, in existence a document in the family of Karl Amenda, an acco mplished amateur who was an intimate friend of Beethoven, which relates the following anecdote:

Beethoven was frequently embarrassed for money. Once he complained to Amenda that he had to pay rent

Beethoven died in his fifty-eighth year in 1827. Some of his contemporaries regarded him, as has already been said, as a violator of all the sacred canons of art. Berlioz denounces Haydn for speaking of him as being merely a great pianist. But while some of his compositions were looked upon as strange and incomprehensible his noble character and resplendent genius were not unrecognized. Twenty thousand persons crowded into the square in front of the house in Vienna from which the funeral procession wended its way to the Trinity Church of the Minorites.

Beethoven was not a radical in the iconoclastic sense of that word, but he avowedly strove to be a modernist, for he himself said that "Freedom, progress is the aim of the world of art as in the whole great universe." But progress must be made, he believed, with deliberation and a just respect for traditional conventions. He once defended the use of consecutive fifths in one of his own compositions, but told the pupil with whom he was discussing this primary law of the theory of music, that while it was allowable for him, Beethoven, to transgress the law, the pupil must observe it until he had demonstrated that he was capable of improving it. Only the greatest poets can safely ignore the

limitations of prosody. Beethoven was in reality
a great poet. He employed music not merely
for the purpose of exciting æsthetic emotions
but to express spiritual experiences. Bekker
calls attention to the fact that on the title page
of one of his overtures he inscribed the statement not that it had been "composed" but
that it had been "made into poetry by Ludwig
van Beethoven."

Beethoven's intellect comprehended more than
the power to express imagination and emotion
through the harmony of sounds. He often
discussed philosophical problems and on one
occasion put an end to a fruitless debate with the
phrase: "Perhaps the reverse may be true."
This gave rise to an interesting incident in the
life of Brahms. Brahms, who was a devout
disciple of Beethoven, discovered the phrase in a
rare manuscript of the great symphonist and
"was fond of using it," says the editor of the
Brahms-Herzogenberg correspondence, "to dispose of any sophistries and equivocations at-
tributed to the philosophers of the day." He
used it once most effectively. Elizabet von
Herzogenberg wrote to Brahms of Nietzsche,
whom they both knew:

I am always lamenting that such an intellect should
have gone to the wrong man. For I do think him ex-

tremely clever despite all his vagaries, his paradoxes and his boundless exaggerations I have seldom been so fascinated by any book as by his *Genealogie der Moral*, for instance, and I would rather disagree with one of his calibre than agree with many others who are more orthodox but who have less to say.

Then, mentioning *Janseits von Gut and Böse* (in which Nietzsche combats the accepted views of Good and Evil), she continues:

His remarks on music . . . are incredible and incomprehensible in relation to the rest. . . . Really this man's vanity will bring him to a lunatic asylum yet!

—a prophecy which came true. Brahms replied:

Don't waste too much precious daylight in reading such things, and remember the saying, "The reverse may be true."

Thus we owe to Beethoven the most complete and satisfactory answer that can be made to the abnormal speculations of the half-crazy Nietzsche. It is as effective as whole volumes of metaphysics.

Beethoven is a kind of miracle—a creative genius to be ranked with Shakespeare and Lincoln. It is amazing that the bitter experiences of his life did not make him a cynic. Yet he has been justly called a poet of deep joy and faith, of "heavenly serenity and repose," to use Thayer's expressive phrase. The lives of few great men so substantiate the assertion of poets and mystics that man possesses a mysterious something called "soul" which is totally unexplained by anatomy, biology, or physiological psychology. The origin of creative genius is one of the great mysteries of life, quite as great as the mystery of the atom, the electron, the ovum, or the spermatozoon. The adherents of heredity and the champions of environment may argue as much as they like, but neither heredity nor environment explain the transcendent spiritual gifts of Shakespeare, Beethoven, and Lincoln. Almost everything in their birth and upbringing might have been expected to destroy greatness of mind and nobility of spirit. Yet the sublimity of their genius grows with time. What process of scientific analysis can explain the Thirtieth Sonnet, or the Fifth Symphony, or the Second Inaugural? All three compositions are most truly supernatural—without progenitors or descendants.

GEORGE STEPHENSON

THE PHILOSOPHER

THE PHILOSOPHER

IT MAY seem incongruous that the son of a Northumberland coal miner, who could neither read nor write until he was nearly twenty years of age and whose speech was marked to the day of his death by the burr or accent of his native county, should be introduced into this company of men of letters and philosophers. But George Stephenson, although he is often spoken of as merely a glorified mechanic, was preëminently a philosopher in one of the most important senses of that term. A few years after his death an English periodical, the *National Review*, discussing the theory of stored-up power in coal, in an article which bore the technical title of "The Phasis of Force," remarked:

We cannot but feel an increased admiration of the intuitive sagacity of that remarkable man, George Stephenson, who was often laughed at for propounding in a somewhat crude form the very idea which we have been endeavouring to present under a more philosophical aspect.

The thought that coal is bottled sunlight is a commonplace of plant biologists to-day, but in Stephenson's time it was an original conception. His biographer, Samuel Smiles, tells the story of Stephenson's first announcement of his theory. Stephenson's locomotives and railways had revolutionized transportation and he had become one of the prominent citizens of England. Sir Robert Peel, one of the finest of England's Prime Ministers, had invited Stephenson to his place, Drayton Manor, to meet a distinguished company. Among the guests was Dr. William Buckland, then famous as a geologist, although he was a clergyman and was a little later appointed Dean of Westminster. Buckland and Stephenson fell into an amiable controversy over the formation of coal, in which Stephenson was the admitted victor.

One Sunday [says Smiles], when the party had just returned from Church, they were standing together on the terrace near the hall, and observed in the distance a railway train flashing along, throwing behind it a long line of white steam. "Now, Buckland," said Mr. Stephenson, "I have a poser for you. Can you tell me what is the power that is driving that train?" "Well," said the other, "I suppose it is one of your big engines." "But what drives the engines?" "Oh, very likely a canny Newcastle driver." "What do you say to the light of the sun?" "How can that be?" asked the doctor. "It is nothing else," said the engineer: "it is light bottled up in the earth for tens of thousands of years—light, absorbed by plants and vegetables for the condensation of carbon during the process of their growth, if it be not carbon in another form—and now, after being buried in the earth for long ages in fields of coal, that latent light is again brought forth and liberated, made to work, as in that locomotive, for great human purposes."

Here speaks the philosopher. In our day the word philosopher has come, in popular parlance, to have a limited meaning. We take it in its Platonistic sense as dealing with abstract thought, and consider Socrates, Spinoza, Kant, Hegel, Spencer, and Bergson to be typical philosophers. A hundred years ago the word was used in the Aristotelian meaning which included all science, both metaphysical and physical. Within this definition Benjamin Franklin was a philosopher quite as well as William James. In the first quarter of the last century, my grandfather held the chair of Mathematics and Natural Philosophy at Amherst College with the munificent annual salary of seven hundred and fifty dollars which was given to him with the understanding that he was to use part of it to keep his "philosophical apparatus" in good condition. No one would include him nowadays in a list of philosophers, unless, perhaps, a third definition of the term were applied to him. In the language of the street a philosopher is a man who takes the ups and downs of life with equanimity and good temper. Stephenson was a notable philosopher in this sense.

The steam railroad is so indispensable an element in modern civilization that we are prone to accept it as a gift of nature, like food and clothing, and hardly realize that it is only a hundred years old. Jefferson and Marshall, like Herodotus, travelled in the saddle or on wheels, and it is because there were no railroads that, when the office of President of the United States was established, Inauguration Day was placed four months after Election Day. Four months was not then too long a time to spend in assembling the members of a newly elected government in the capital of so vast a territory as that formed by the original thirteen states. The birthday of steam transportation on land was the 27th of September, 1825. This was the date of the public opening of the Stockton and Darlington Railway, in the north of England, on which, for the first time, a locomotive was used to draw passengers and freight over metal rails. On this occasion, a stationary engine pulled the loaded cars or wagons up the steepest incline or grade and lowered them on the other side. At the foot of the grade a "travelling engine" was coupled on and driven by George Stephenson, whose first experimental locomotive had been successfully operated ten years earlier and whose immortal "Rocket" was not built until five years later. The Stockton and Darlington train consisted of thirty-four open wagons—the first six loaded with coal and flour, next a special coach for the directors of the company and their friends, then twenty-one wagons with temporary seats for ordinary passengers, and at the end of the train six more wagons loaded with coal. "The signal being given," says a contemporary observer, "the engine started off with its immense train of carriages, and such was its velocity, that in some parts the speed was frequently as much as twelve miles an hour; and at that time the number of passengers was counted to be four hundred and fifty, which, together with the coals, merchandise, and carriages, would amount to near ninety tons!"

The exclamation mark is my own. To-day in the United States the heaviest engines and tenders alone weigh considerably over two hundred tons, and freight trains of over two thousand tons are not unknown. No one can read, even superficially, the history of steam-railroad transportation without feeling that George Stephenson is one of the very great figures in the history of modern civilization.

In a hundred years, the mileage of the railroads of the world, exclusive of trams and trolleys, has grown from less than one hundred miles to approximately seven hundred thousand miles. And yet, says the biographer of George Stephenson,

the idea of travelling at a rate of speed double that of the fastest mail coach appeared at that time so preposterous that Mr. Stephenson was unable to find any engineer who would risk his reputation in supporting his "absurd views." . . . George Stephenson's scheme was indeed at that time regarded but as the dream of a chimerical projector. It stood before the public friendless, and scarcely daring to lift itself into notice for fear of ridicule. The civil engineers generally rejected the notion of a Locomotive Railway; and when no leading man of the day could be found to stand forward in support of the Killingworth mechanic, its chances of success must have been pronounced but small.

The idea would have had no chance at all if it had not been for Stephenson's indomitable faith and persistence. He had as opponents all of the university and technical savants, most of the landed aristocracy, and even the government itself—for Parliament frowned upon his plans. The *Quarterly Review*, established by the great publisher John Murray as a rival to the *Edinburgh Review*—the two periodicals exercising an influence upon the controlling thought of Great

Britain which has no parallel in our day—said of Stephenson's plan:

What can be more palpably absurd and ridiculous than the prospect held out of locomotives travelling *twice as fast* as stage coaches! We should as soon expect the people of Woolwich to suffer themselves to be fired off upon one of Congreve's ricochet rockets, as to trust themselves to the mercy of such a machine going at such a rate.

This was written when Sir Walter Scott was one of the mainstays of the *Quarterly* and Macaulay was a shining light of the *Edinburgh Review*.

In his History of England, notably in the famous third chapter, Macaulay pays more attention to the material progress and welfare of the people than any other historian—so much so that Emerson said of him: "The brilliant Macaulay, who expresses the tone of the English governing classes of the day, explicitly teaches that 'good' means good to eat, good to wear, material commodity." It is a commentary on the habitual tendency of the intellectuals to ignore the achievements of the industrials that Macaulay apparently took little interest in the enormous economic and political changes which Stephenson and the railways produced in England. Macaulay joined the staff of the *Edinburgh Review* a few weeks after the installation

poor for that. At fifteen years of age he was assistant fireman on a stationary engine at the mouth of a coal pit, earning a shilling a day, and his highest ambition was to become an engine-man. He was eighteen years old before he even learned to read. But genius has its own methods of obtaining an education. Having learned to read, and at nineteen to write his own name, he began to take lessons in arithmetic at a night school conducted by a Scotsman, paying his teacher fourpence a week. The value which he set upon education is shown by what he did for his own son, Robert, who later became an accomplished engineer and his father's partner and associate.

In the earlier period of my career [Stephenson once said in a public speech], when Robert was a little boy, I saw how deficient I was in education, and I made up my mind that he should not labour under the same defect, but that I would put him to a good school, and give him a liberal training. I was, however, a poor man; and how do you think I managed? I betook myself to mending my neighbours' clocks and watches at nights, after my daily labour was done, and thus I procured the means of educating my son.

In accordance with the definite design of Stephenson, the son contributed to the father's education without knowing it. The process reminds one of the Pasteur family, where a reverse method was followed. Louis Pasteur tactfully helped his father's intellectual progress without letting the father know what he was doing; George Stephenson tactfully availed himself of his boy Robert's schooling without giving the boy an inkling of what was going on. Robert, says Stephenson's biographer,

was entered a member of the Newcastle Literary and Philosophical Institution, the subscription to which was £3. 3s. a year. He spent much of his leisure time there, reading and studying; and on Saturday afternoons when he went home to his father's at Killingworth, he usually carried with him a volume of the *Repertory of Arts and Sciences*, or of the *Edinburgh Encyclopædia*, which furnished abundant subjects for interesting and instructive converse during the evening hours. Then John Wiggham would come over from the Glebe farm to join the party, and enter into the lively scientific discussions which occurred on the subjects of their mutual reading. But many of the most valuable works belonging to the Newcastle Library were not permitted to be removed from the room; and these Robert was instructed to read and study, and bring away with him descriptions and sketches for his father's information. His father also practised him in the reading of plans and drawings without referring at all to the written descriptions. He used to observe to his son, "A good drawing or plan should always explain itself"; and, placing a drawing of an engine or machine before the youth, he would say, "There, now, describe that to me—the arrangement and the action." Thus he taught him to read a drawing as easily as he would read a page of a book. And this practice soon gave to both the greatest facility in apprehending the details of even the most difficult and complicated mechanical drawing.

It will thus be seen that, although he never went to a technical school, or to an organized school of any kind, Stephenson's education as a mechanical engineer was much more intellectual than one of the rule of thumb. Even before his marriage he used to model stationary engines in clay, and when he became an engineman it was his habit to take his own engine to pieces in order to become familiar with its mechanism. It was not long before he achieved a local reputation as a skilled mechanic, and many were the wheezy and leaky pumping engines, unable because of defects to keep their coal pits clear of water, which he cured.

He was, of course, familiar as a boy with so-called "rail-ways." As early as 1676, in the neighbourhood of Newcastle, wooden rails were laid from the mouth of the coal pits, and wagons on wheels which fitted these wooden rails were drawn by horses. Next, in order to protect the wooden rails from rotting and wear, thin plates of iron were nailed upon them. Then cast-iron rails were substituted for the wooden ones and cast-iron flanges were fastened to the wagon tires to keep the wheels upon the track. In the year

1800 one Benjamin Outram substituted stone props for wooden sleepers in the horse railroads used at the coal mines. His invention was called an "Outram road" which was finally shortened to "tram road," whence sprang the words "tram" and "tramcar," used in England to this day.

The first idea of steam locomotion was to have a steam-propelled vehicle use ordinary carriage roads for its path. It is said that a Frenchman was imprisoned in a madhouse by the authorities in 1641 because of the importunities with which he plagued them to listen to a description of an invention for propelling ships at sea and moving carriages on land by steam. In 1772, an American, Oliver Evans by name, invented a steam carriage for common roads, but it was never practically developed.

I have already alluded to the singular indifference of the English historians and men of letters in the early part of the Nineteenth Century to the problem of steam transportation, the solution of which by George Stephenson was about to revolutionize the civilized world. Political controversies, not scientific experimentation, occupied their attention. There is one notable exception. George Borrow, the author of those three fine English classics, *The Bible in Spain*,

Lavengro and *The Romany Rye*, had his eye upon the steam coach. Borrow at sixteen was articled for five years to a firm of solicitors in Norwich, but languages and literature interested him much more than the law. In 1824, having reached the age of twenty-one and thus having escaped from his irksome legal apprenticeship, he went up to London and became hack writer for the newspapers. It was then, just the year before the opening of the Stockton and Darlington Railway, that Borrow wrote an article or essay on the steam coach, the original manuscript of which, in the handwriting of Borrow, is one of the items in the notable collection of Mr. Alba Boardman Johnson of Philadelphia, formerly president of the Baldwin Locomotive Works. Although the essay is slightly sophomoric in style, for Borrow had not yet struck his gait, I reprint it in full with Mr. Johnson's permission; for it shows how unfamiliar England was with the work of Stephenson and how totally unprepared Englishmen were for the transformation of economic and industrial life which was so soon to burst upon them:

It is very difficult at the present moment to procure any satisfactory information respecting steam coaches and their success, the columns of the newspapers being so closely crowded with political matter. This much is known, however, that a steam coach occasionally runs upon the Brighton road, a road the surface of which being very unequal is well calculated to demonstrate the practicability or impracticability of locomotive vehicles running on all kinds of ground. Hitherto the locomotive carriage has been in its infancy, and though no doubt can be entertained by an impartial mind as to the ultimate success and universal adoption of this species of conveyance, some period must elapse in England before the utility and expediency are generally proclaimed and recognized. It is decried with great fury and treated with contempt though perhaps affected by most of those individuals who are in any degree connected with or interested in upholding the old system, namely, of horse carriage conveyance, and many people who do not choose to be troubled with thinking for themselves have suffered their minds to be prejudiced by ex parte statements and verbiage, which with some may pass for argument but which I feel no inclination to dignify with that name. One favourite point of dispraise amongst the enemies of locomotive carriages, and the only one which can be considered worthy of observation, for all the rest that is said against it is not worthy of repetition or the slightest comment, is that these machines cannot surmount hills, and notwithstanding it has been satisfactorily proved that this objection is utterly unfounded, they nevertheless for want of something better to say and having nothing else which is not infinitely more absurd, still echo and re-echo it. I shall take the liberty of saying a few words on this point, though I must confess it scarcely merits them, which will show to the dullest understanding how vastly contrary to fact and nature such an assertion must be. True it is, and every one knows that by the law of gravitation it is more difficult for everything but a fly to move upwards than downwards, and that if a body is to move with the same velocity up a hill as it does down the hill, a far greater degree of force must be exerted. Now no one ever was foolish enough to suppose that a steam coach which moves along a level at the rate of 16 miles an hour would be able to surmount a steep hill with the same degree of velocity with the same propelling power, but admitting that a steam coach can move along a level at the rate of 16 miles an hour, which nobody can deny, and requires a force far greater than that which propells any horse coach at present running, what reason in the world is there that that steam coach should not surmount the hill with greater speed than any horse coach in the world? Some people doubtless from obstinacy, will say that it cannot, but by so doing they stake themselves on the horns of an absurdity, for though the power of steam like the power of animals is to a certain degree impeded by uphill work, the steam power being greater than the animal power in all cases the ascent must consequently be accomplished with less difficulty. But to abandon this part of the subject, no one ventures to deny the wonderful facility with which steam coaches run over level ground, and as the road from New York to Albany is throughout one unbroken level, not the shadow of an objection can be made against forthwith starting a steam vehicle upon it. An undertaking of this description would be subjected to much less difficulty and impediment in America than in Great Britain where innovation of every kind is generally dreaded and decried by a vast number of persons whose interest compels them to wish the old order of things continued. As every great road in England is crowded with coaches worked by horses, each of which coaches carries many individuals, can it be wondered at that a scheme which threatens to take away the bread from many people's mouths and which tends to render a hitherto valuable species of property but of slight value, can it be wondered at that such a scheme is subjected to much scoffing and abuse? But all this will doubtless soon pass away. Indeed I was told lately by one of the proprietors of a Norwich coach that he had no doubt that in five years steam coaches would be on every principal road in England and horse public coaches almost as great a rarity as steam coaches are now.

Stephenson appears to have been the first to work seriously upon the conception of a locomotive to run upon "rail-ways." At all events, he was the first to believe that the power of adhesion would drive a smooth-wheeled engine upon a smooth rail, and in 1814 he built such an engine for the "rail-way" at a coal mine at Killingworth. The principal partner in the mine was Lord Ravensworth, who backed Stephenson financially in building his locomotive. The machine worked satisfactorily, and in honour of his financial backer Stephenson named it "My Lord." Fifteen years later, at the age of forty-eight, Stephenson built the first practical passenger locomotive in a contest for a prize of $2,500 offered by the promoters of the Liverpool and Manchester Railway. This was the famous *Rocket*, which embodied all the general principles of the modern locomotive, notably the forced draft created by sending the exhaust steam through the smokestack. The *Rocket* is now preserved at Newcastle as a memento of Stephenson. It deserves such preservation, for it is the grandfather, with an immense progeny, of all the locomotive engines in the world.

Stephenson was not merely a man of one idea. He was an amateur naturalist of no mean pretensions; he invented a safety lamp for miners, which was called in his honour by his enthusiastic co-workers the "Geordy," although it was superseded by the more perfect appliance invented by Sir Humphrey Davy; he was a civil engineer as well as a great mechanic; indeed, his range of interests was so wide that Ralph Waldo Emerson, who met him in England in 1847, just before his death, spoke of him as one who "had the lives of many men in him." Unlike many inventors Stephenson reaped the well-earned rewards of his own labours and discoveries. His last years he spent on his well-equipped country estate leading "the life of a country gentleman of ample means," and taking great delight in the pineapples, melons, cucumbers, and other fruits and vegetables which he grew with great success. A letter extant but I think unpublished, written four years before his death, reveals in a pleasant fashion his love of horticulture as well as his humorous philosophy:

Tapton House
Julv 26th, 1844.

My dear Sir:

I hope you and Mrs. Hardcastle got safe home. Mrs. Stephenson expected to have met you at the station as you passed. She had unfortunately looked up the wrong time table and only got down to the bottom of the park when the train passed. She had a basket of strawberries for your party, which would have served you eating I think all the way to Newcastle, and a most beautiful melon for old Mrs. Hardcastle, which came under my management after dinner, and I assure you it was most luxurious.

Mrs. Stephenson is delighted with her bonnet, but on.y think of two pounds for such a thing! I suppose a nice straw bonnet might have been got for 5 or 8 shillings. What a waste of money for taste, and taste for what? for something for people to look at, that you do not care one fig about. Comfort and decency ought to be considered and nothing more. But I suppose from the time of Eve coaxing Adam to eat the forbidden fruit she engendered into her off-spring the *controlling* power over man, and I suppose we must quietly bend to their wishes, to attempt to turn them is like turning the tide in the ocean. However notwithstanding all their faults they can certainly soothe man when the world frowns upon him and I suppose it is best to let them go on having their own way to a moderate degree. But only think of *two pounds* for a bonnet!!

I am my dear sir

Yours truly
Geo. Stephenson.

Wm. Hardcastle, Esqr.

In his youth Stephenson was an athlete. His biographer describes a fight, under prize-ring rules, which he had when he was twenty years old with a fellow coal labourer who was the bully and the terror of the village:

Great was the excitement at Black Callerton when it was known that George Stephenson had accepted Nelson's challenge. Everybody said that he would be killed. The villagers—the young men, and especially the boys of the place, with whom George was an especial favourite—all wished that he might beat Nelson, but they scarcely dared to say so. They came about him while he was at work in the engine house, to inquire if it was really true that he was "goin' to feight Nelson?" "Aye; never fear for me; I'll feight him." And "feight him" he did. For some days previous to the appointed day of battle, Nelson went entirely off work for the purpose of keeping himself fresh and strong; whereas Stephenson went on doing his daily work as usual, and appeared not in the least disconcerted by the prospect of the affair. So, on the evening appointed, after George had done his day's labour, he went into the Dolly Pit Field, where his already exulting rival was ready to meet him. George stripped, and "went in" like a practised pugilist—though it was his first and last battle. After a few rounds, George's wiry muscles and practised strength enabled him severely to punish his adversary, and to secure for himself an easy victory.

This was an affair that might have pleased George Borrow, whose famous apostrophe to the "bruisers of England" in *Lavengro* even so fastidious a critic as Sir Augustine Burrell calls "as good as Homer."

Stephenson, in his old age, if one may judge

from his portrait, was a handsome figure of a man. Extremely popular with the hundreds of working men who were his associates and employees and held in high regard by men of the highest social position, he was always characterized by self-respect and modest self-possession. More than once offered a knighthood by the Prime Minister, Sir Robert Peel, he courteously but persistently declined the honour. He had no need of the title, nor has his memory need of the tribute it was intended to convey. As plain George Stephenson he will be, as he ought to be, long remembered in the list of the great philosophical benefactors of mankind.

RALPH WALDO EMERSON

THE HUMOURIST

him, of course—that he was a mystical philosopher; the apostle of transcendentalism in America; a somewhat obscure stylist; a poet of the loftiest ideas whose forms of expression are so compact and elliptical that he often out-Brownings Browning; and, above all, of such serenity of mind and soul that he sometimes seems like an embodied spirit from another world. I have owned a definitive edition of Emerson's works for twenty years, the collection edited and published by his son, but I confess that I have not often taken a volume down from its shelf for entertaining reading. On a recent occasion, however, I was confined to my room for a few days by a sharp attack of lumbago. Now, if there is ever a time when a man wants serenity it is in the midst of one of these annoying visitations of the imps of pain. In desperation I turned to Emerson, and discovered to my joy that he was one of the most delightful of humourists.

Where he got his sense of humour is hard to tell. Perhaps it was not born in him but was acquired by experience, for his face in early portraits is aloof-looking, while the most famous of his photographs, taken when he was seventy years of age, is the best portrayal of a gentle, kindly, and intelligent sense of humour I have ever seen. His son tells us that as a boy and young man he was intensely shy. This shyness, combined with a New England conscience, led him to give up the Unitarian ministry when he was about thirty years of age, and for the remaining fifty years of his life he devoted himself to writing and lecturing. That he had a New England conscience is indicated by the remark he once made about conversation with bores. "I had," he said, "as lief talk with my own conscience." He has left his own estimate of the value of a sense of humour. "What an ornament and safeguard is humour! Far better than wit for the poet and writer. It is genius itself, and so defends from the insanities."

In this estimate is a lesson for the fundamentalists who are just now insisting upon the acceptance of certain metaphysical doctrines which have been artificially wrought into the Church by nineteen centuries of argumentative theologians who, whatever may have been their other virtues, certainly lacked the virtue of a sense of humour. What an uncompromising insistence on a literal creed leads to is amusingly pointed out by Emerson in his *English Traits*. The religion of the Church of England, he says, fosters among the English a belief

which does not treat with levity a pound sterling; they are neither transcendentalists nor Christians; they put up no

Socratic prayer, much less any saintly prayer for the Queen's mind; ask neither for light nor right; but say bluntly, "Grant her in health and wealth long to live."

But after this delicate and smiling thrust Emerson goes on to say:

Yet, if religion be the doing of all good, and for its sake the suffering of all evil, *souffrir de tout le monde, et ne faire souffrir personne*, that divine secret has existed in England from the days of Alfred to those of Romilly, of Clarkson and of Florence Nightingale, and of thousands who have no fame.

Only one who possesses a sense of humour can define its functions and effects. I do not know of a better definition than that which Emerson gave in his eulogy of Abraham Lincoln:

Then his broad good humour, running easily into jocular talk, in which he delighted and in which he excelled, was a rich gift to this wise man. It enabled him to keep his secret; to meet every kind of man and every rank in society; to take off the edge of the severest decisions; to mask his own purpose and sound his companion; and to catch with true instinct the temper of every company he addressed. And, more than all, it is to a man of severe labour, in anxious and exhausting crises, the natural restorative, good as sleep, and is the protection of the overdriven brain against rancour and insanity.

Emerson's writings are full of allusions, analogies, and bits of kindly satire that could come only from a man who saw the little incongruities as well as the nobilities and tragedies of life. But I think the outstanding example of his combination of humour with deep spiritual appreciation is the portrait of Socrates in his essay on "Plato the Philosopher"—an essay of which Carlyle said that it had little of value for him "save Socrates with his clogs and big ears." To save the reader the trouble of seeking it out on his own shelves or the shelves of a public library I quote it here in full:

Socrates, a man of humble stem, but honest enough; of the commonest history; of a personal homeliness so remarkable as to be a cause of wit in others:—the rather that his broad good nature and exquisite taste for a joke invited the sally, which was sure to be paid. The players personated him on the stage; the potters copied his ugly face on their stone jugs. He was a cool fellow, adding to his humour a perfect temper and a knowledge of his man, be he who he might whom he talked with, which laid the companion open to certain defeat in any debate—and in debate he immoderately delighted. The young men are prodigiously fond of him and invite him to their feasts, whither he goes for conversation. He can drink, too; has the strongest head in Athens; and after leaving the whole party under the table, goes away as if nothing had happened, to begin new dialogues with somebody that is sober. In short, he was what our country-people call *an old one*.

He affected a good many citizen-like tastes, was monstrously fond of Athens, hated trees, never willingly went beyond the walls, knew the old characters, valued the bores and philistines, thought everything in Athens a little better than in any other place. He was plain as a Quaker in habit and speech, affected low phrases, and illustrations from cocks and quails, soup-pans and sycamore-spoons, grooms and farriers, and unnamable offices—especially if he talked with any superfine person. He had a Franklin-like wisdom. Thus he showed one who was afraid to go on foot to Olympia, that it was no more than his daily walk within doors, if continuously extended, would easily reach.

Plain old uncle as he was, with his great ears, an immense talker,—the rumour ran that on one or two occasions, in the war with Bœotia, he had shown a determination which had covered the retreat of a troop; and there was some story that under the cover of folly, he had, in the city government, when one day he chanced to hold a seat there, evinced a courage in opposing singly the popular voice which had well-nigh ruined him. He is very poor; but then he is hardy as a soldier, and can live on a few olives; usually, in the strictest sense, on bread and water, except when entertained by his friends. His necessary expenses were exceedingly small, and no one could live as he did. He wore no under garment; his upper garment was the same for summer and winter, and he went barefooted; and it is said that to procure the pleasure, which he loves, of talking at his ease all day with the most elegant and cultivated young men, he will now and then return to his shop and carve statues, good or bad, for sale. However that be, it is certain that he had grown to delight in nothing else than this conversation; and that, under his hypocritical pretense of knowing nothing, he attacks and brings down all the fine speakers, all of the fine philosophers of Athens, whether natives or strangers from Asia Minor or the islands. Nobody can refuse to talk with him, he is so honest and so really curious to know; a man who was willingly confuted if he did not speak the truth, and who willingly confuted others asserting what was false; and not less pleased when confuted than when confuting; for he thought not any evil happened to men of such a magnitude as false opinion regarding the just and the unjust.   A piti-less disputant, who knows nothing, but the bounds of whose conquering intelligence no man has ever reached; whose temper was imperturbable; whose dreadful logic was always leisurely and sportive; so careless and ignorant as to disarm the wariest and draw them, in the pleasantest manner, into horrible doubts and confusion.   But he al-ways knew the way out; knew it, yet would not tell it. No escape; he drives them to terrible choices by his dilem-mas, and tosses the Hippiases and Gorgiases with their grand reputations, as a boy tosses his balls.   The tyran-nous realist, Meno, has discoursed a thousand times, at length, on virtue, before many companies, and very well, as it appeared to him; but at this moment he cannot even tell what is his,—this cramp-fish of a Socrates has so be-witched him.

This hard-headed humourist, whose strange conceits, drollery, and *bonhomie* diverted the young patricians, whilst the rumour of his sayings and quibbles gets abroad every day—turns out, in the sequel, to have a probity as invincible as his logic, and to be either insane, or at least, under cover of this play, enthusiastic in his religion.   When accused before the judges of subverting the popular creed, he affirms the immortality of the soul, the future reward and punishment; and refusing to recant, in a caprice of the popular government was condemned to die, and sent to the prison.   Socrates entered the prison and took away all ignominy from the place, which could not be a prison whilst he was there.   Crito bribed the jailer; but Socrates would not go out by treachery.   "Whatever inconvenience ensue, nothing is to be preferred before justice.   These things I hear like pipes and drums, whose sound makes me deaf to everything you say." The fame of this prison, the fame of the discourses there and the drinking of the hemlock are one of the most precious passages in the history of the world.

The rare coincidence, in one ugly body, of the droll and the martyr, the keen street and market debater with the sweetest saint known to any history at that time, had forcibly struck the mind of Plato, so capacious of these contrasts; and the figure of Socrates by a necessity placed itself in the foreground of the scene, as the fittest dispenser of the intellectual treasures he had to communicate. It was a rare fortune that this Æsop of the mob and this robed scholar should meet, to make each other immortal in their mutual faculty.

Where in American literature can there be found on so compact a canvas a portrait lined in more beautiful English or illumined with a more delightful humour?

Emerson was born in Boston in 1803 the son of a Unitarian minister and with a singularly ministerial ancestry. He could count among his progenitors many zealous preachers of the church. The line goes back into England where one of them, a Fellow of St. John's College, Cambridge, and a rector of the Church of England, got into difficulty because of his liberal views, fled to New England, and was one of the founders of the town of Concord with which Ralph Waldo Emerson's name is ever associated. However liberal might have been the theological views of the New England Unitarians, their attitude toward life was austere enough. Emerson's great-grandfather, a minister, a graduate of Harvard and a great scholar for his day, believed, like St. Francis of Assisi, in poverty and would have nothing to do with a near relative, "who had a grant of land, and was rich." This great-grandfather "prayed every night that none of his descendants might ever be rich." His father believed in rigorous training. Once when away from home he wrote to his wife, says James Cabot, Ralph Waldo's biographer:

William [aged five] will recite to you as he does to me, if you have leisure to hear him, a sentence of English grammar before breakfast,—though I think, if only one can be attended to, Ralph [aged three] should be that one.

And he "hopes that John Clarke [aged seven] can repeat passages from Addison, Shakespeare, Milton, Pope, etc." Emerson came legally by the discriminating appreciation of British culture which appears in his book on *English Traits* published in 1856. Of his mother, who was born in Massachusetts when that state was an English colony, he wrote to an unidentified friend, in 1853, in a letter which may be found in a charming collection published by Charles Eliot Norton:

My little household is grown much less by the loss of my mother. She was born to live. She lived eighty-four years, yet not a day too long, and died suddenly and unexpectedly at the last. She was born a subject of King George, was bred in the Church of England, and, though she had lived through the whole existence of this nation, and was tied all round to later things, English traditions and courtesies and the Book of Common Prayer clung to her in her age, and, had it been practicable, it would have seemed more fit to have chanted the Liturgy over her, and buried her in her father's tomb under Trinity Church.

Emerson, a Unitarian and a thoroughgoing Yankee, with a mother who was an Episcopalian and typically English!

Emerson's aunt, a remarkable character, when he left the Church and became a transcendental philosopher, "quarrelled with him for his 'high, airy speculations,' and would not see him or even come into the town where he was." Nevertheless, he wrote of her:

Give my love to her,—love and honour. She must always occupy a saint's place in my household; and I have no hour of poetry or pholosophy, since I knew these things, into which she does not enter as a genius.

It is easy to see where Emerson acquired that shyness and reserve which the world has taken for austerity. At Harvard, which he entered a few months after his fourteenth birthday he had, says a classmate,

the same manner and courtly hesitation in addressing you
that you have known in him since. Emerson was not
talkative; he never spoke for effect; his utterances were well
weighed and very deliberately made; but there was a
certain flash when he uttered anything that was more than
usual worthy to be remembered.

He was chosen Class Poet by his class, and
toward the end of his life was given the degree of
LL.D by Harvard and elected to its Board of
Overseers. The only political office which he
ever held was that of hog-reeve of the Town of
Concord, a questionable honour which was thrust
upon him without his knowledge. On leaving
college he taught for a while in a school conducted by his brother, studied divinity and became a minister successively of two of the leading Unitarian churches of Boston.

The Unitarians of those days were the intellectual leaders of New England. A contemporary of Emerson's, "Tom" Appleton, a famous
wit of his day, once differentiated the Unitarians
from the Universalists by saying "that the
Universalists are a body of people who think that
God is too good to damn them, while the Unitarians are a body of people who think that they
are too good for God to damn." Emerson left
the Unitarian body not because he thought they
were too good, but because he could not endure

to be circumscribed by even the liberal forms and rites of that ecclesiastical organization. He once wrote, "If I should go out of church whenever I hear a false sentiment I should never stay there five minutes." He was calmly but intensely individualistic and was compelled by his inner genius to express himself and himself only. After he left the pulpit the rest of his life, interrupted by three visits to Europe, was spent in Concord, of which he became the recognized sage and where he devoted himself to writing his voluminous lectures and essays. On his European visits, he met in England the great intellectual and literary personages of the time and formed a notable friendship with Carlyle. To a non-philosophical reader like myself his book *English Traits* is the most interesting of his productions, as good as any novel. He was happily married twice and was a devoted husband and father in spite of the fact that, in his private journal, he once semi-humorously advocated celibacy:

If I judge from my own experience [he wrote] I should unsay all my fine things, I fear, concerning the manual labour of literary men. They ought to be released from every species of public or private responsibility. To them the grasshopper is a burden. I guard my moods as anxiously as a miser his money; for company, business, my own household chares [old English for chores], untune and disqualify me for writing. I think then the writer ought not to be married; ought not to have a family. I think the Roman Church with its celibate clergy and its monastic cells, was right. If he must marry, perhaps he should be regarded happiest who has a shrew for a wife [Socrates was evidently in his mind], a sharp-tongued notable dame who can and will assume the total economy of the house, and, having some sense that her philosopher is best in his study, suffers him not to intermeddle with her thrift. He shall be master but not mistress, as Elizabeth Hoar said.

And yet he records, with apparent approval, the fact that "Sam Ward says, 'I like women, they are so finished.'" Again the following tribute to woman appears in his Journal:

Woman should not be expected to write, or fight, or build or compose scores; she does all by inspiring man to do all. The poet finds her eyes anticipating all his ode, the sculptor his god, the architect his house. She looks at it. She is the requiring genius.

His paternal instinct was strong. The entries in his Journal about the death of his boy reveal a deep side of his nature, and his experience is comparable to that of Darwin and Pasteur under similar bereavements.

January 28, 1842.

Yesterday night, at fifteen minutes after eight, my little Waldo ended his life.

January 30.

The morning of Friday, I woke at three o'clock, and every cock in every barnyard was shrilling with the most unnecessary noise. The sun went up the morning sky with all his light, but the landscape was dishonoured by this loss. For this boy, in whose remembrance I have both slept and awaked so oft, decorated for me the morning star, the evening cloud, how much more all the particulars of daily economy; for he had touched with his lively curiosity every trivial fact and circumstance in the household, the hard coal and the soft coal which I put into my stove; the wood, of which he brought his little quota for grandmother's fire; the hammer, the pincers and file he was so eager to use; the microscope, the magnet, the little globe, and every trinket and instrument in the study; the loads of gravel on the meadow, the nests in the hen-house, and many and many a little visit to the dog house and to the barn. . . . A boy of early wisdom, of a grave and even majestic deportment, of a perfect gentleness. Every tramper that ever tramped is abroad, but the little feet are still. He gave up his little innocent breath like a bird.

February 21.

Home again from Providence to the deserted house. Dear friends find I, but the wonderful Boy is gone. What a looking for miracles have I! As his walking into the room where we are would not surprise Ellen [the boy's small sister], so it would seem to me the most natural of all things.

June 16.

Charles King Newcomb is a Religious Intellect. Let it be to his praise that when I carried his manuscript story to the woods, and read it in the armchair of the upturned root of a pine tree, I felt for the first time since Waldo's death some efficient faith again in the repairs of the universe, some independencies of natural relations whilst spiritual affinities can be so perfect and compensating.

Like all humourists, Emerson, while not at all moody, was a man of varying moods. His private Journal, published in several volumes, justifies this assertion. I know of nothing in diarial literature, not even Pepys's immortal work, which is quite such a revelation as this Journal of the innermost reactions and impressions of an individual mind and spirit. As the purpose of this sketch is not to discuss Emerson's place in the world of letters as a philosopher, poet, moralist, and abstract thinker, but to point out his too little recognized humorous attitude toward life, I shall simply quote without special arrangement or reasoning some extracts from this Journal which have struck me as I have turned its leaves.

Of the opera he says:

In town I also heard some admirable music. It seemed, as I groped for the meaning, as if I were hearing a history of the adventures of fairy knights,—some Wace, or Monstrelet, or Froissart, was telling in a language which I very imperfectly understood, the most minute and laughable particulars of the tournaments and loves and quarrels and religion and tears and fate of airy adventurers, small as moths, fine as light, swifter than shadows,—and these anecdotes were illustrated with all sorts of mimicry and scene-painting, all fun and humour and grief, and, now and then, the very persons described broke in and answered and danced and fought and sung for themselves.

What expert musical critic, reporting for a modern newspaper, could do anything more true or entertaining than this!

In his early life, Emerson was a great admirer, almost a worshipper, of the powerful intellect of Daniel Webster. He had regarded Webster as "the one eminent American of our time whom we could produce as a finished work of nature?" But Webster's course toward slavery and the South seemed to Emerson to be "treachery." Following his journal entry about the opera, he has this to say:

I saw Webster on the street,—but he was changed since I saw him last,—black as a thundercloud, and careworn. . . . I did not wonder that he depressed his eyes when he saw me, and would not meet my face. The canker-worms have crawled to the topmost bough of the wild elms and swung down from that. No wonder the elm is a little uneasy.

A few pages later he relates this anecdote:

"What are you doing, Zeke?" said Judge Webster to his eldest boy.
"Nothing."
"What are you doing, Daniel?"
"Helping Zeke."
A tolerably correct account of most of our activities to-day.

There were flappers in those days, and Emerson explained them exactly as they might be explained now:

The young people complain that everything around them must be denied, and therefore, if feeble, it takes all their strength to deny, before they can begin to lead their own life. Aunt Betsey and Uncle Gulliver insist on their respect to this Sabbath and that Rollin's History or Fragment Society or some other school, or charity, or morning call, which, to preserve their integrity, they resist.

This was written more than eighty years ago!

In discussing with a Concord neighbour, a Unitarian clergyman, the unconventionalists or non-conformists or radicals of those days, and on this neighbour's declaring, with the optimism of the conservative, that there were very few of such folk, Emerson records his reply:

I told him he was like the good man of Noah's neighbours who said, "Go to thunder with your old ark! I don't think there'll be much of a shower."

This bit of humour recalls two or three entries on profanity.   He reports that two friends gave him

an amusing account of a truckman who came to the [Harvard] college yard and bullied for an hour; it was the richest swearing, the most æsthetic, fertilizing,—and they took notes.

A little later on he observes:

Swearing has gone out of vogue on the earth, because society, which means discriminating persons, rejects unmeasured speech. Oaths never go out of fashion, but are always beautiful and thrilling; but the sham of them, which is called profane swearing, is rightly voted a bore. Sham damns we do not like.

Yet again he says:

What a pity that we cannot curse and swear in good society! Cannot the stinging dialect of the sailors be domesticated? It is the best rhetoric, and for a hundred occasions those forbidden words are the only good ones. My page about "Consistency" [the essay in which he said that consistency is the hobgoblin of little minds] would be better written thus: Damn Consistency!

Emerson had a humorous appreciation of some of the characteristics of the simpler sort of his Yankee neighbours:

The Yankee is one who if he once gets his teeth set on a thing, all creation can't make him let go; who, if he can get hold anywhere of a rope's end or a spar, will not let it go, but will make it carry him; if he can but find so much as a stump or a log, will hold on to it and whittle out of it a house and barn, a farm and stock, a mill-seat and a village, a railroad and a bank, and various other things equally useful and entertaining—a seat in Congress or a foreign mission, for example. But these no doubt are inventions of the enemy.

In the letters published by Charles Eliot
Norton, there is a quizzical comment on the
Yankee village of Concord:

What can I tell you?   Not the slightest event enlivens
our little sandy village; we have not even rigged out a hay
cart for a whortleberry party.   If I look out of the window
there is perhaps a cow; if I go into the garden there are
cucumbers; if I look into the brook there is a mud turtle.
In the sleep of the great heats there was nothing for me but
to read the Vedas, the bible of the tropics, which I find I
come back upon every three or four years.   It is sublime
as heat and night and a breathless ocean.

The same series of letters includes an amusing
one written from Philadelphia:

Philadelphia, I fancied, was a great unit, a less New
York, if not so large and populous, more majestic, a city of
rich repose.   But after conversing now with many persons
here for a few days, I cannot find at all any city, any unit.
A great multitude of houses, all nearly alike, lying very
peacefully together—but the tenants, from their number,
very much unknown to each other, and not animated by
any common spirit, or by the presence of any remarkable
individuals.   In the absence of the usual excitements of
trade, the whole body certainly wears a very lymphatic
appearance; one might call it, but for the disrespect to the
divine sex, a very large granny.   For there seems an entire
absence here of any strenuous men or man or public
opinion; a deference to the opinion of New York; a fear
of Boston; and, in this great want of thought, a very dull
timidity and routine among the citizens themselves.   I
have diligently enquired among the intelligent for the

more intelligent; asked every Greek, "who was the second best in the camp?" yet have found no Atrides. Very fair and pleasant people, but thus far, no originals. If the world was all Philadelphia, although the poultry and dairy market would be admirable, I fear suicide would exceedingly prevail.

Emerson especially enjoyed the rugged humour of one of his Concord neighbours. The philosopher's son, the editor of the Journal, thus describes this Yankee character in whom Emerson found a basis for real friendship:

He [Emerson] told them [Bronson Alcott and another friend] of an engagement at noon to marry some young people at the Middlesex Tavern. The bridegroom was Samuel Staples, then bartender, and the bride the landlord's daughter. This good man, three years later, in his official capacity, arrested for refusal to pay taxes Alcott, Thoreau and Charles Lane, the English friend of the former and held two of them in jail until ransomed by friends. It should be said that he offered to pay Thoreau's tax himself, but this Thoreau would not allow. Having come to Concord a boy, with a few pence in his pocket and begin as hostler, Mr. Staples rose through the grades of bartender, clerk, constable and jailer, deputy sheriff, representative to the General Court, auctioneer, real-estate agent, and gentleman farmer to be one of the most valued and respected fathers of the village family. In Mr. Emerson's last years, Mr. Staples was his next neighbour and good friend, and came affectionately to bid him good-bye in the last hours of his life. He once was commenting to a friend of the family on the number of visitors that came, some of them from beyond the seas, and added, "Well, I suppose there's a great many things that Mr. Emerson knows that I couldn't understand; but I *know* that there's a damn sight of things that I know that he don't know anything about."

A man of letters and an habitual associate of books Emerson sometimes felt that there was such a thing as too much literacy.

Byron says of Jack Bunting [he comments], "He knew not what to say, and so he swore." I may say it of our preposterous use of books, He knew not what to do, and so *he read.*

Doubtless he was familiar with the bookish sprees of the poet Gray—"Elegy" Gray—who, says Edmund Gosse, was in the "habit of drowning consciousness in perpetual study," and used "to plunge into an excess of reading, treating the acquisition of knowledge as a narcotic." With history of the so-called scientific or chronological school he apparently had little sympathy if one may judge from this entry:

There is no history. There is only Biography. The attempt to perpetrate, to fix a thought or principle, fails continually. You can only live for yourself; your action is good only whilst it is alive, whilst it is in you. The awkward imitation of it by your child or your disciple is not a repetition of it, it is not the same thing, but another thing. The new individual must work out the whole problem of science, letters, and theology for himself; can owe his fathers nothing. There is no history; only biography.

Still another entry gives Emerson's evaluation of biography:

To find a story which I thought I remembered in *Quentin Durward*, I turned over the volume until I was fairly caught in the old foolish trap and read and read to the end of the novel.   Then, as often before, I feel indignant to have been duped and dragged after a foolish boy and girl, to see them at last married and portioned, and I instantly turned out of doors like a beggar that has followed a gay procession into the castle.   . . .

Yet a novel may teach one thing as well as my choosings at the corner of the street which way to go,—whether to my errand or to the woods,—this, namely, that action inspires respect; action makes character, power, man, God.

These novels will give way, by and by, to diaries or autobiographies;—captivating books, if only a man knew how to choose among what he calls his experiences that which is really his experience, and how to record truth truly!

The pomps and ceremonies even of the intellectual world amused him:

At Dartmouth College, last July, was a good sheriff-like gentleman with a loud voice, a pompous air, and a fine coat, whose aid, it seemed, the College annually called in, to marshal their procession.   He was in his element; he commanded us all with such despotic condescension, as put all dignities and talents but his own quite aside.   He marched before, the College followed him like a tame dog.

Emerson did not always live in the clouds. He had some regard for the material side of life, as this entry in his Journal testifies:

This afternoon I found Edmund Hosmer in his field, after traversing his orchard where two of his boys were grafting trees; Mr. Hosmer was ploughing and Andrew driving the oxen. I could not help feeling the highest respect as I approached this brave labourer. Here is the Napoleon, the Alexander of the soil, conquering and to conquer, after how many and many a hard-fought summer's day and winter's day, not like Napoleon of sixty battles only, but of six thousand, and out of every one he has come victor. . . . I am ashamed of these slight and useless limbs of mine before this strong soldier.

Perhaps it was Emerson's realization that his spirit outweighed his body which led him to note, with an apparent chuckle, a saying of his wife's: "Queenie says, 'Save me from magnificent souls. I like a small common-sized one.'"

One of the interesting episodes in Emerson's career was the establishment by George Ripley, a Harvard graduate and a Unitarian minister, of Brook Farm, that curious and short-lived experiment in intellectual communism which so aroused the enthusiasm of the New England transcendentalists and literary lights. With Ripley were associated such men as Charles A. Dana, later the brilliant and uncommunistic owner and editor of the New York *Sun*, and George William Curtis, who afterward made *Harper's Weekly* a power in journalism. Ripley himself was finally associated with the New

York *Tribune* as one of its editors. Emerson
was urged by Ripley to become a charter member
of the new community, but he fought shy of
organized transcendentalism. "At the name
of a society," he said, "all repulsions play, all
my quills rise and sharpen," and he made the
following entry in his Journal:

Yesterday George and Sophia Ripley, Margaret Fuller,
and Alcott discussed here the new social plans. I wished
to be convinced, to be thawed, to be made nobly mad by
the kindlings before my eye of a new dawn of human
piety. But this scheme was arithmetic and comfort; a
hint borrowed from the Tremont House and the United
States Hotel; a rage in our poverty and politics to live
rich and gentlemanlike; an anchor to leeward against a
change of weather. And not once could I be inflamed but
sat aloof and thoughtless; my voice faltered and fell. It
was not the cave of persecution, which is the palace of
spiritual power, but only a room in the Astor House hired
for the Transcendentalists.

His sense of humour saved him from being
made ludicrous, for Brook Farm, although conceived on a high plane and with fine ideals, was
an object of good-natured raillery and finally
fell to pieces from its own unsubstantiality.
Emerson saw through it at the beginning and
understood why he was urged to join the enter-
prise; for, a year or two later, when the visionary
community was sliding down hill, he observes:

Ellery [doubtless William Ellery Channing, a minor poet and nephew of the great Dr. Channing] says that at Brook Farm they keep Curtis and Charles Newcomb and a few others as decoy-ducks.

Emerson's range of interests was very wide and his tastes very catholic. He thought about and commented on art, science, metaphysics, travel, invention, education, industrialism. He was engaged in intently watching the progress of mankind and anything that affected that progress enlisted his attention. It is striking to find that seventy-five years ago he foresaw with his mind's eye the molecular researches which are just now so deeply engaging the thought of chemists and physicists. "This new molecular philosophy," he wrote in his Journal in May, 1842, "goes to show that there are astronomical interspaces betwixt atom and atom; the world is all outside; it has no inside.

> Atom from atom yawns as far
> As moon from earth, as star from star."

There is no humour in this, but there is in his picture of the railroads which were just then beginning to grow and extend themselves in the United States—a dry New England humour like that which prompted Emily Dickinson's unusual poem on the railroad train. Said Emerson:

I hear the whistle of the locomotive in the woods. Wherever that music comes it has its sequel. It is the voice of the civility of the Nineteenth Century saying, "Here I am." It is interrogative: it is prophetic: and this Cassandra is believed: "Whew! Whew! Whew! How is real estate here in the swamp and wilderness? Ho for Boston! Whew! Whew! Down with that forest on the side of the hill. I want ten thousand chestnut sleepers. I want cedar posts, and hundreds of thousands of feet of boards. Up! my masters of oak and pine! You have waited long enough—a good part of a century in the wind and stupid sky. Ho for axes and saws, and away with me to Boston! Whew! Whew! I will plant a dozen houses on this pasture next moon, and a village anon; and I will sprinkle yonder square mile with white houses like the broken snowbanks that strow it in March."

Best of all, Emerson's sense of humour was broad enough to include amusement over his own supposed defects. Daniel Chester French, the sculptor of the Minuteman, modelled a bust of Emerson when the humorous philosopher was seventy-six years of age. The sculptor wrote to Emerson's biographer a few years after the bust was completed the following letter:

I think it is very seldom that a face combines such vigour and strength in the general form and plan with such exceeding delicacy and sensitiveness in the details. Henry James somewhere speaks of "the over-modelled American face." No face was ever *more* modelled than was Mr. Emerson's; there was nothing slurred, nothing accidental; but it was like the perfection of detail in great sculpture;

it did not interfere with the grand scheme. Neither did it interfere with an almost child-like mobility that admitted of an infinite variety of expression, and made possible that wonderful "lighting-up" of the face so often spoken of by those who knew him. It was the attempt to catch that glorifying expression that made me despair of my bust. At the time I made it, as you know, Mr. Emerson had failed somewhat, and it was only now and then that I could see, even for an instant, the expression I sought. . . . When the bust was approaching completion he looked at it after one of the sittings, and said, "The trouble is, the more it resembles me the worse it looks."

So one could go on piling up quotation after quotation from this gentle but very modern humourist to indicate his kindly attitude toward life. Few philosophers have done more to help the average man to bear the little burdens and irritations of daily life with equanimity.

CHARLES R. DARWIN

THE SAINT

TEN: CHARLES R. DARWIN

THE SAINT

born 1809—died 1882

GAMALIEL BRADFORD, the American biographer, has recently published an essay which he entitles "Darwin the Destroyer" and which he closes with these sorrowful words: "It was Darwin who at least typified the rigorous logic that wrecked the universe for me and for millions of others."

If Gamaliel Bradford's conception of the universe was that of the ancient Hebrews—a geocentric machine operated by an anthropomorphic God—then there is cause for his lament. I cannot share it, although I suppose I was brought up in as pure an atmosphere of New England orthodoxy as he was. It may be admitted that Darwin is the destroyer of the geocentric-anthropomorphic theology. But I regard him as a saint, for he has substituted for a ghastly mechanism a universe which is illimitable in its truth, beauty, and mystery; and truth, beauty, and mystery are the attributes of the highest form of religion.

Far from being a rank materialist Darwin seems to me to have been something of a mystic. The deeper he penetrated into the secrets of nature, the greater the mystery became. In his sixty-fifth year he wrote to a Dutch student·

I may say that the impossibility of conceiving that this grand and wondrous universe, with our conscious selves, arose through chance, seems to me the chief argument for the existence of God; but whether this is an argument of real value, I have never been able to decide. . . . The safest conclusion seems to me that the whole subject is beyond the scope of man's intellect; *but man can do his duty*.

The italics are mine. I underscore the words because they are the key to his perhaps sombre but surely saintlike spirit. The note of sadness that occasionally sounds in his private letters and conversation is due to his loss of the comfortable gnosticism or know-it-allness which was characteristic of the University where he had been educated, of the circles of friends and relations that was dear to him, of the Church whose splendid ritual he had so often repeated, and of the very government under which he lived as a loyal citizen. He said more than once that he had no wish or intent to destroy any other man's faith, but as for himself he must pursue the truth wherever it led him. It required the spirit of a saint to follow this course, without apology or self-defense, in spite of the abuse, denunciation, and slander that were dashed upon his gentle head. Happily for those who loved him, he had a champion in his devoted friend Huxley who delighted to do battle for him and who did not shrink from hitting even a bishop's head occasionally with as beautifully handled and intellectual shillalah as was ever swung in a debate.

The *Origin of Species*, the work in which Darwin first announced his doctrine of evolution, was published late in 1859. In June, 1860, a famous meeting at Oxford of the British Association was the arena for a pitched battle over Darwin's new theory quite as exciting and vehement as the recent contest at Dayton, Tennessee, in which the late Mr. Bryan was the most prominent gladiator. About the only difference is that at Oxford the contestants were either educated scientists or University men while at Dayton the stage was occupied largely by ignoramuses. Bishop Wilberforce, who was popularly known because of his specious rhetorical eloquence as "Soapy Sam," was the Bryan of the occasion. He proceeded to "smash Darwin," and Huxley in turn smashed him. The story is fully told in the biography of Huxley by his son Leonard. The excitement was intense. "One lady," said an observer, "fainted and had to be carried out; I, for one, jumped out of my seat." The fundamentalists and the modernists were egged on by the cheers of their partisans. In the peroration of his attack, the Bishop is said by the Rev. Dean Freemantle to have spoken as follows:

"I should like to ask Professor Huxley who is sitting by me, and is about to tear me to pieces when I have sat down, as to his belief in being descended from an ape. Is it on his grandfather's or his grandmother's side that the ape ancestry comes in?" And then taking a graver tone, he asserted, in solemn peroration, that Darwin's views were contrary to the revelation of God in the Scriptures.

Darwin was not present but Huxley was called upon to reply. Turning to a friend before he rose he said *sotto voce*, "The Lord hath delivered into mine hands." Dean Freemantle reports him as beginning:

I am here only in the interest of science and I have not heard anything which can prejudice the case of my august client.

After completely exposing the Bishop's scientific incompetency, Huxley continued, according to John Richard Green, then an Oxford undergraduate but later the distinguished English historian:

I asserted—and I repeat—that a man has no reason to be ashamed of having an ape for his grandfather. If there were an ancestor whom I should feel shame in recalling it would rather be a man—a man of restless and versatile intellect—who, not content with an equivocal success in his own sphere of activity, plunges into scientific questions with which he has no real acquaintance, only to obscure them by an aimless rhetoric, and distract the attention of his hearers from the real point at issue by eloquent digressions and skilled appeals to religious prejudice.

Intellectual England was torn asunder by this debate, but gradually the operations of quiet reason prevailed and the principle of evolutionary progress in the processes of nature was accepted both in Church and University. This happened more than half a century before the furor in Tennessee. It only shows how far behind we are in the procession. Huxley's attachment to Darwin was based not merely on scientific sympathy but on admiration for his essential goodness. Three weeks after Darwin's death Huxley wrote to a friend who was common to them both:

"Colossal" does not seem to me to be the right epithet for Darwin's intellect. He had a clear, rapid intelligence, a great memory, a vivid imagination, and what made his greatness was the strict subordination of all these to his love of truth.

And in September of the year of the Oxford meeting, a letter from Huxley to his friend Charles Kingsley, protesting against the "hard names" of atheist and infidel which were applied to Darwin and himself, contains these phrases:

The ledger of the Almighty is strictly kept, and everyone of us has the balance of his operations paid over to him at the end of every minute of his existence. . . . And thus, my dear Kingsley, you will understand what my position is. I may be quite wrong, and in that case I know I shall have to pay the penalty for being wrong. But I can only say with Luther, *"Gott helfe mir, ich kann nichts anders."* . . . One thing people shall not call me with justice and that is—a liar.

Darwin's life conforms to the definition of the religious spirit once made by that other scientific saint, President Charles W. Eliot, who said that the distinctive fruits of religion are "love, reverence, and duty." One may go even further and believe that Darwin displayed the real spirit of the Christian religion if we accept Dr. Eliot's interpretation:

What then is the renewed Christianity which these terrible times we are living in cry out for in the midst of tears and heartbreaking sorrows? It is a Christianity which abandons the errors and the unjust, cruel conceptions which the centuries have piled up on the simple teachings of Jesus. It is a Christianity which sympathizes with and supports the aspirations of mankind for freedom—freedom in thought, speech and action—and completely abandons authoritative ecclesiasticism and governmental despotism.

It is a Christianity which hallows and consecrates birth, marriage, the bringing up of children, family life, the earning of a livelihood, . . . and rejects all the aspersions on the natural life of man which Christianity inherited from paganism and Judaism.

It is a Christianity which will be the friend and ally of all that is good and ennobling in literature, science and art, and will avail itself without fear of all the new means of teaching and helping men which successive generations shall discover, and of all the innocent enjoyments and social pleasures, while resisting effectively every unwholesome or degrading influence on human society.

It is a Christianity which will recognize that the pursuit of happiness in this world is legitimate for every human being, and that the main function of government is to protect and further men in that pursuit by securing to the community health, education, wholesome productive labour and liberty.

I make no attempt to appraise or interpret the doctrine of evolution. The origin of man, if not the origin of species is still a physical and metaphysical mystery. But no thinking person now questions the biological fact that in nature there is a law of development from a lower to a higher order. Darwin, if not the first to suspect the existence of this law, was the first to investigate it deliberately and state it scientifically. It is not this, however, that impels me to include him in the company gathered together in this volume. His personal qualities, his methods of work, and his attitude toward life are what have enlisted my interest and admiration.

The year 1809 might be marked with red on the calendar, for it was the birth year of three great modernists—Lincoln, Gladstone, and Darwin. Darwin came from a family of intellectuals. His great-great-great-grandfather was a barrister and loyalist in the time of Oliver Cromwell; his great-grandfather, also a barrister, was a man of property who lived a life of leisure ameliorated by dabblings in amateur science; his paternal grandfather was a physician by education, a botanist by inclination, and a poet by main strength; his maternal grandfather was the famous English ceramist, Josiah Wedgwood; his father was a highly respected physician with a very large practice, an uncanny gift for diagnosis, and was so good a judge of investments that he left his children a comfortable fortune. Darwin often referred to his father as "the wisest man I ever knew" and said of him in his reminiscences:

My father's mind was not scientific, and he did not try to generalize his knowledge under general laws; yet he formed a theory for almost everything which occurred. I do not think I gained much from him intellectually, but his example ought to have been of much moral service to all his children. One of his golden rules (a hard one to follow) was, "Never become the friend of anyone whom you cannot respect."

What were some of the moral qualities which he derived from his father and what were some of his standards of respect for others is disclosed in a naïve and engaging fashion in his private letters and journals. In them may be discovered his generous appreciation of others, his sense of humour, his modest estimate of his own ability, and his capacity for the tenderest family affection. Describing Robert Brown, a famous botanist of his day, he alludes to the fact that this Scotch curator of the botanical section of the British Museum was "strangely jealous" of the discoveries of other scientists and reluctant to reveal to them his own. However, Darwin adds:

He was capable of the most generous actions. When old, much out of health, and quite unfit for any exertion, he daily visited (as Hooker told me) an old manservant who lived at a distance (and whom he supported), and read aloud to him. This is enough to make up for any degree of scientific penuriousness or jealousy.

A fine tribute to the soundness of the cup-of-cold-water test of essential goodness!

For a ruthless destroyer, Darwin had a delightful sense of humour. He reports that once, at an evening party, he met Buckle, whose *History of Civilization* went up like a rocket and came down like a stick. Buckle talked so incessantly that he, Darwin, hardly attempted to say a word. Buckle afterward said in the presence of Darwin's brother, "Well, Mr. Darwin's books are much better than his conversation." Stanhope the historian, better known as Lord Mahon, was a friend of Darwin. Through him Darwin met his somewhat eccentric father, "the old Earl," who took a fancy to the budding young scientist and turning to him one day said, "Why don't you give up your fiddle-faddle of geology and zoology, and turn to the occult sciences?" Young Stanhope was somewhat shocked at his father's brusqueness, but Darwin and the historian's "charming wife" were much amused. Darwin knew Macaulay and Carlyle. Macaulay he liked and says, contrary to contemporary opinion, that "he did not talk at all too much"; Carlyle was antipathetic to him partly because Carlyle once said to him that his friend Grote's history was "a fetid quagmire, with nothing spiritual about it," and partly because Carlyle's mind was "so ill-adapted for scientific research." Darwin admits that Carlyle was "all-powerful in impressing some grand moral truths on the mind of man," but he found that "his views about slavery were revolting," that "in his eyes might was right," and that "his mind seemed to me a very narrow one." He tells an amusing incident about Carlyle and the mathematician Babbage:

The last man whom I will mention is Carlyle, seen by me several times at my brother's house, and two or three at my own house. His talk was very racy and interesting, just like his writing, but he sometimes went on too long on the same subject. I remember a funny dinner at my brother's, where, amongst a few others, were Babbage and Lyell [the great geologist], both of whom liked to talk. Carlyle, however, silenced everyone by haranguing during the whole dinner on the advantages of silence. After dinner Babbage, in his grimmest manner, thanked Carlyle for his very interesting lecture on silence.

One incident will suffice to reveal Darwin's beautiful tenderness. His daughter Annie, a child of ten years, died. Within a few days of her death he wrote down these impressions of her:

I write these few pages, as I think in after years, if we live, the impressions now put down will recall more vividly her chief characteristics. From whatever point I look back at her, the main feature in her disposition which at once rises before me, is her buoyant joyousness, tempered by two other characteristics, namely, her sensitiveness, which might easily have been overlooked by a stranger, and her strong affection. Her joyousness and animal spirits radiated from her whole countenance, and rendered every movement elastic and full of vigour. It was delightful and cheerful to behold her. Her dear face now rises before me, as she used sometimes to come running downstairs with a stolen pinch of snuff for me, her whole form radiant with the pleasure of giving pleasure. . . . She would at almost any time spend half an hour in arranging my hair, "making it," as she called it, "beautiful," or in smoothing, the poor dear darling, my collar or cuffs—in short, fondling me.

She was in her manners remarkably cordial, frank, open, straightforward, natural, and without any shade of reserve. Her whole mind was pure and transparent. One felt one knew her thoroughly and could trust her. I always thought, that come what might, we should have had in our old age at least one loving soul which nothing could have changed. . . . In her last short illness her conduct in simple truth was angelic. She never once complained; never became fretful; was ever considerate of others, and was thankful in the most gentle, pathetic manner for everything done for her. When so exhausted that she could hardly speak, she praised everything that was given her, and said some tea "was beautifully good." When I gave her some water she said, "I quite thank you"; and these, I believe, were the last precious words ever addressed by her dear lips to me.

We have lost the joy of our household, and the solace of our old age. She must have known how we loved her. Oh, that she could now know how deeply, how tenderly, we do still and shall ever love her dear joyous face! Blessings on her!

A prayer for the dead from the destroyer of religion!

The futility of some phases of the old-fashioned classical education is patent in Darwin's case. From school he was sent to Edinburgh University, his father's idea being to make a doctor of him. Here he got some insight into geology and zoology but discovered that medicine did not appeal to him. This was perhaps because, as he said in later life, the lectures on materia medica and anatomy were so "incredibly dull" as to be "fearful to remember." Drawing and dissection, which would have been of inestimable value to him in his life career, were neglected by his teachers or advisers; so were French and German. These four essentials he had to pick up as well as he could by himself in his adult years. As he appeared to be a misfit at Edinburgh, it was decided to prepare him for the Church, a plan into which he entered dutifully if not enthusiastically, so he went to Cambridge. Of this period of his life he says with a touch of humour:

Considering how fiercely I have been attacked by the orthodox, it seems ludicrous that I once intended to be a clergyman. Nor was this intention and my father's wish ever formally given up, but died a natural death when, on leaving Cambridge, I joined the *Beagle* as a naturalist. If the phrenologists are to be trusted, I was well fitted in one respect to be a clergyman. A few years ago the secretaries of a German psychological society asked me earnestly by letter for a photograph of myself; and some time afterwards I received the proceedings of one of the meetings, in which it seemed that the shape of my head had been the subject of a public discussion, and one of the speakers declared that I had the bump of reverence developed enough for ten priests.

What really happened to change his choice of a career was, that his instinctive interest in science swamped his interest in theology. He spent his spare time in collecting beetles. "No pursuit at Cambridge," he says, "was followed with nearly so much eagerness or gave me so much pleasure." Although in his old age he looked back to his three years at Cambridge as "wasted," so far as intellectual progress was concerned, his life there was normal and happy and he probably got a good deal more out of it than he realized. He had warm friends, was a member of a popular dinner club and was devoted to snipe and grouse shooting. This latter sport he gave up while still an undergraduate for a characteristic reason.

Before he left Cambridge [said a college friend in some recollections of Darwin], he told me that he had made up his mind not to shoot any more; that he had had two days' shooting at his friend's, Mr. Owen of Woodhouse; and that on the second day, when going over some of the ground that they had beaten the day before, he picked up a bird not quite dead, but lingering from a shot it had received the previous day; and that it had made and left such a painful impression on his mind, that he could not reconcile it to his conscience to continue to derive pleasure from a sport which inflicted such cruel suffering.

The same friend continues:

I cannot end this cursory and rambling sketch without testifying, and I doubt not all his surviving college friends would concur with me, that he was the most genial, warm hearted, generous and affectionate of friends; that his sympathies were with all that was good and true; and that he had a cordial hatred for everything false, or vile, or cruel, or mean, or dishonourable. He was not only great, but preëminently good, and just, and lovable.

Curiously enough, while at Cambridge, Darwin frequented a musical set and used to time his walks so as to hear on weekdays the anthem in King's College Chapel. I once heard the anthem sung in that incomparable building by the men's choir without the accompaniment of the organ, which had temporarily broken down, and I can easily appreciate the profound impression which that superb music must have made on Darwin. I allude to Darwin's early taste for music as being curious because, late in life, he deplored the fact that it had become wholly atrophied from disuse. He seems, however, to have overlooked the fact that his early familiarity with music had its influence in his investigations of the origin of species. In a letter which he wrote to the German naturalist, Fritz Müller, during the controversies in the scientific as well as the religious world about his theories, he said:

> I have often reflected with surprise on the diversity of means for producing music with insects, and still more with birds. We thus get a high idea of the importance of song in the animal kingdom.

That this importance was a mystery to him not to be explained merely by the laws of biology and heredity, he intimates in another letter to the English psychologist Edmund Gurney:

> I never supposed that the different degrees and kinds of pleasure derived from different music could be explained by the musical powers of our semi-human progenitors. Does not the fact that different people belonging to the same civilized nation are very differently affected by the same music, almost show that these diversities of taste and pleasure have been acquired during their individual lives? [That is to say, there are qualities of the *ego* which cannot be explained by physical science.] Your simile of architecture seems to me particularly good; for in this case the appreciation must be almost individual, though possibly the sense of sublimity excited by a grand cathedral may have some connection with the vague feelings of terror and superstition in our savage ancestors, when they entered a great cavern or gloomy forest. I wish someone could analyze the feeling of sublimity.

Darwin valued the æsthetic side of man's nature and deplored what he supposed was his own deficiency in this respect. I quote the following rather long passage from the private journal written for his children because it gives his opinion of the importance of the relation of art to science and reveals his own genuine humility:

Up to the age of thirty, or beyond it, poetry of many kinds, such as the works of Milton, Gray, Byron, Wordsworth, Coleridge, and Shelley, gave me great pleasure, and even as a schoolboy I took intense delight in Shakespeare, especially in historical plays. I have also said that formerly pictures gave me considerable, and music very great delight. But now for many years I cannot endure to read a line of poetry: I have tried lately to read Shakespeare, and found it so intolerably dull that it nauseated me. I have also almost lost my taste for pictures or music. Music generally sets me thinking too energetically on what I have been at work on, instead of giving me pleasure. I retain some taste for fine scenery, but it does not cause me the exquisite delight which it formerly did. On the other hand, novels which are works of the imagination, though not of a very high order, have been for years a wonderful relief and pleasure to me, and I often bless all novelists. A surprising number have been read aloud to me, and I like all if moderately good, and if they do not end unhappily—against which a law ought to be passed. A novel, according to my taste, does not come into the first class unless it contains some person whom one can thoroughly love, and if a pretty women all the better. [The modern Main Street school of novelists will please take notice!]

This curious and lamentable loss of the higher æsthetic tastes is all the odder as books on history, biographies, and travels (independent of any scientific facts they may contain), and essays on all sorts of subjects interest me as much as ever they did. My mind seems to have become a kind of machine for grinding general laws out of large collections of facts, but why this should have caused the atrophy of that part of the brain alone, on which the higher tastes depend, I cannot conceive. A man with a mind more highly organized or better constituted than mine, would not, I suppose, have thus suffered; and if I had my life to live again, I would have made a rule to read some poetry and listen to some music at least once every week; for perhaps the parts of my brain now atrophied would thus have been kept active through use. The loss of these tastes is a loss of happiness, and may possibly be injurious to the intellect, and more probably to the moral character, by enfeebling the emotional part of our nature.

This scientific reference to the emotional side of man's nature is hardly a fair measure of the part which the emotions played in Darwin's life. Underneath his calm and equable exterior some very deep feelings seethed although he kept them under control. He was a contemporary of John Bright and Gladstone, but I cannot find any record in his letters of special interest in the political reforms—the abolition of the Corn Laws and the extension of the franchise, for example— which tore England asunder during his young manhood and made world figures of Bright and Gladstone. He did, however, align himself with John Bright on the question of slavery, which he had learned to detest during his visit on the *Beagle* to Brazil just after he left Cambridge. G. M. Trevelyan, in his life of John Bright, notes the fact that Darwin and Huxley supported the committee, in which John Bright was a leader, organized for the prosecution of the notorious Governor Eyre whose cruel treatment of the Negroes in the island of Jamaica had roused the better sentiment of England. Carlyle ranged himself on the other side as a supporter of imperial authority, thus confirming Darwin's early judgment, already noted, that he was an upholder of the doctrine that might makes right. How deeply the feelings of England were stirred at this time, especially the feelings of the common people, appears in an incident related by Trevelyan:

More than a generation after the Corn Laws had been repealed, a great Liberal meeting was advertised in Manchester with Lord Hartington in the chair, and Bright as chief speaker. Before the proceedings began, a gentleman in the audience found himself sitting behind three old workingmen who had walked in from a neighbouring county to hear John Bright speak once more, because they had often heard him in the Corn Law days. When they saw him come on to the platform they all three broke down and burst into tears.

Darwin shared in the emotional experience through which England then passed. While he did not burst into tears he did, in private, burst into passionate language more than once that suggests the moral fury of an Old Testament prophet. At the outbreak of our Civil War, he wrote to Asa Gray, the distinguished botanist at Harvard:

I never knew the newspapers so profoundly interesting. North America does not do England justice; I have not seen nor heard of a soul who is not with the North. Some few, and I am one of them, even wish to God, though at the loss of millions of lives, that the North would proclaim a crusade against slavery. In the long run, a million horrid deaths would be amply repaid in the cause of humanity. What wonderful times we live in! Massachusetts seems to show noble enthusiasm. Great God! how I should like to see the greatest curse on earth—slavery—abolished. Farewell.

Darwin undoubtedly overemphasized the atrophy of his emotions and underestimated his æsthetic tastes, for his son says that, up to the end of his life, he greatly enjoyed parts of Beethoven's symphonies and showed discrimination in his appreciation of the style of different musical performers. A year before his death, Hans Richter, the celebrated German orchestral conductor, paid a visit to Darwin at his home, "Down House," in the county of Kent, and Richter's playing on the piano aroused Darwin to unwonted enthusiasm.

Of Darwin's scientific achievements and career it is not necessary to speak here. The record in outline may be found in any good encyclopædia. He began it by enlisting at the age of twenty-two as naturalist on the famous voyage of the *Beagle*, whose five-year voyage in the waters of South America, the South Sea Islands, and Australasia, laid the basis for his epoch-making contribution, *The Origin of Species*, to the sciences of zoology, botany, entomology, and anthropology. Not only that, his hypotheses and demonstrations, founded upon the most meticulous study and observation, changed the whole current of modern thought in history, philosophy, and theology. His scientific hypotheses may be superseded, but his influence on the human mind can never be eradicated. The sources of this influence he has himself endeavoured to analyze. The analysis is characterized by his habitual simplicity, modesty, and search for the truth:

I have no great quickness of apprehension or wit, which is so remarkable in some clever men, for instance, Huxley. I am therefore a poor critic: a paper or book, when first read, generally excites my admiration and it is only after considerable reflection that I perceive the weak points. My power to follow a long and purely abstract train of thought is very limited; and therefore I could never have succeeded with metaphysics or mathematics. . . .

Some of my critics have said, "Oh, he is a good observer,

but he has no power of reasoning!" I do not think this can be true, for the *Origin of Species* is one long argument from the beginning to the end, and it has convinced not a few able men. No one could have written it without having some power of reasoning. I have a fair share of invention, and of common sense or judgment, such as every fairly successful lawyer or doctor must have, but not, I believe, in any higher degree.

On the favourable side of the balance, I think that I am superior in noticing things which easily escape attention, and in observing them carefully. My industry has been nearly as great as it could have been in the observation and collection of facts. What is far more important, my love of natural science has been steady and ardent.

This pure love has, however, been much aided by the ambition to be esteemed by my fellow naturalists. From my early youth I have had the strongest desire to understand or explain whatever I observed—that is, to group all facts under some general laws. These causes combined have given me the patience to reflect or ponder for any number of years over any unexplained problem. As far as I can judge, I am not apt to follow blindly the lead of other men. I have steadily endeavoured to keep my mind free so as to give up any hypothesis, however much beloved (and I cannot resist forming one on every subject), as soon as facts are shown to be opposed to it. . . .

My habits are methodical, and this has been of not a little use for my particular line of work. Lastly, I have had ample leisure from not having to earn my own bread. Even ill-health, though it has annihilated several years of my life, has saved me from the distractions of society and amusement.

Therefore my success as a man of science, whatever this has amounted to, has been determined, as far as I can judge, by complex and diversified mental qualities and conditions. Of these, the most important have been—the love of science—unbounded patience in long reflecting over any subject—industry in observing and collecting facts—and a fair share of invention as well as of common sense. With such moderate abilities as I possess, it is truly surprising that I should have influenced to a considerable extent the belief of scientific men on some important points.

One of the most striking tributes to Darwin's elemental goodness comes from an unexpected source which has not yet, I think, found its way into permanent literature. About three years ago there was a movement to purchase Darwin's home, "Down House," as a permanent memorial. At that time I found in the New York *Evening Post* a remarkable letter in behalf of the movement written from Cambridge, England, and signed A. J. Skinner. It reads partly as follows:

I was born and lived within sight of Down House, Darwin's old home. . . . Some of my boyhood years were spent in the service of Charles Darwin, my father being at the same time a coachman in his employ.

Before me as I write is a picture of Down House with its creeper-clad walls, the old-fashioned veranda set about with comfortable chairs, the smooth, velvety lawn with the old sundial and flower beds, and the ancient mulberry tree, whose fruit when ripe was eagerly contended for by a host of noisy blackbirds, thrushes and others of the feathered tribes. I do not, however, require the aid of a photograph to bring back a memory picture of Down House as I knew it, for the old mansion, the gardens and orchard, the paddocks and the long leafy walk, known as the sandwalk, leading to a little coppice and a summer house, are as familiar to me after nearly fifty years as my present surroundings.

Another picture which also comes easily to mind is that of a tall, striking figure in Inverness cape and black, wide-brimmed, soft felt hat, striding along well-kept paths, followed by his inseparable companion, a white fox terrier, which, wandering neither to left nor right, trots steadily a length or so behind his master's heels. We whose duty it was to keep the paths and flower beds free from weeds and rubbish always knew the time of day when we saw the master of Down House approaching, for with him punctuality was a virtue, and the daily walk at the same hour each day was noted by us as an indication of what was expected of those who served him. But although Charles Darwin required punctuality and other virtues in those about him, no employer was more beloved and affectionately regarded, for just dealing and consideration were as much a part of his great nature as was his penetrating scientific mind.

Two little incidents from my own experience may serve to illustrate this fact. I was cutting the lawn one day and at one end of it I spied a queer looking apparatus with metal rods driven through the turf a foot or more into the ground. Being of a curious nature, I couldn't resist pulling up one of the rods to see what it was all about. While examining it I became aware of the presence of someone near, and stealing a guilty glance behind, I was almost paralyzed to see the "master," as we called him, standing over me.

I felt a great relief when I saw a kindly smile and heard a kindly voice saying: "Are you studying earthworms too, my little man? Be careful to put the rod back where it came from."

On another occasion, in the afternoon of a midsummer day, when most of the village lads of my age were playing at cricket or other games, I was weeding one of the main walks. On my knees, hot and irritated, grumbling audibly and stabbing viciously at the weeds, I again became aware of a sympathetic voice saying, "I am sure you find that trying work to-day; finish it some other time," and the first half-crown of my own I ever possessed was pressed into my hand. So, too, the old gardener who tended the greenhouses, where experiments on plants were carried on and who at times may have unknowingly disturbed carefully adjusted instruments and appliances, could if he were alive testify to the same kindly consideration.

Numerous stories of Charles Darwin's thoughtfulness and kindness to man and beast were current among the villagers round about, and keen regrets and concern were felt in many a village home during the time of his fatal illness. One of the saddest days of my life, and I know others of the village folk shared my emotion, was when I set out to the nearest telegraph office, six miles away, with a bunch of telegrams which gave the news to the world that a great and noble heart had ceased to beat.

The full measure of Darwin's achievements cannot be appreciated without taking into account one phase of his life which is sometimes overlooked—his chronic invalidism. Of this his son gives the following brief but remarkable record:

If the character of my father's working life is to be understood, the conditions of ill-health, under which he worked, must be constantly borne in mind. He bore his illness with such uncomplaining patience, that even his children can hardly, I believe, realize the extent of his habitual suffering. In their case the difficulty is heightened by the fact that, from the days of their earliest recollections, they saw him in constant ill-health—and saw him, in spite of it, full of pleasure in what pleased them. Thus in later life, their perception of what he endured had to be disentangled from the impression produced in childhood by constant genial kindness under conditions of unrecognized difficulty. No one, indeed, except my mother, knows the full amount of suffering he endured, or the full amount of his wonderful patience. For all the latter years of his life she never left him for a night; and her days were so planned that all his resting hours might be shared with her. She shielded him from every avoidable annoyance, and omitted nothing that might save him trouble, or prevent him becoming overtired, or that might alleviate the many discomforts of his ill-health. I hesitate to speak thus freely of a thing so sacred as the life-long devotion which prompted all this constant and tender care. But it is, I repeat, a principal feature of his life, that for nearly forty years he never knew one day of the health of ordinary men, and that thus his life was one long struggle against the weariness and strain of sickness. And this cannot be told without speaking of the one condition which enabled him to bear the strain and fight out the struggle to the end.

Huxley says, in his *Darwinia*, that this invalidism was the result of an illness contracted in South America, in 1834, during his memorable voyage on the *Beagle*. Thus he was a martyr as well as a saint.

In this journalistic essay there has been no

endeavour to draw an original portrait of Darwin or to give an estimate of his personality from a new point of view. What has been done is to assemble quotations in a convenient form—chiefly from the memorable biography by his son Francis—which let Darwin's associates speak for him and Darwin speak for himself to those younger American readers who have been told that he was an enemy of the peace and happiness of mankind. How that accusation would have troubled him may be surmised from the fact that he once wrote to a friend quoting the phrase "peace on earth, good will to men" and then adding, "which, by the way, I always think the most perfect description of happiness that words can give."

Francis of Assisi never uttered a more saint-like sentiment.

JEAN FRANÇOIS MILLET

◦◦❖◦◦

THE NATURALIST

ELEVEN: JEAN FRANÇOIS MILLET

THE NATURALIST

BORN 1814—DIED 1875

ON ANY list of interesting modern biographies Alfred Sensier's life of Millet ought to find a place. Sensier was the son of a Paris notary and studied law himself. He did not practise his profession, but was satisfied with a subordinate government office, for his absorbing avocation was the promotion of art of which he made himself an accomplished amateur. He became the friend of the famous group of Barbizon painters—Rousseau, Dupré, Troyon, Diaz, Millet, and their colleagues—but Millet, just of his own age, was his beau ideal. Sensier's biography, delightful in its intimacy, is noteworthy because it portrays the development of a human spirit as well as the technical progress of a great painter. The following sketch of Millet's life is largely based on Sensier's book from which I have ventured to make my own translations, although many quotations have been admirably translated by Julia Cartwright, whose life of Millet is the best extant in English.

Millet was born, of a family of peasant farmers, in the little village of Gruchy near Cherbourg in Normandy. He was christened François after his patron saint, St. Francis of Assisi. Thus, by a coincidence worth noting, a slight thread connects Millet with Voltaire, and both with the Italian saint who loved nature and her beauty.

There is a passage in Millet's own recollections, written at Sensier's request, in which the reader may discern the sources of the artist's love of colour and form as well as of human kindness:

I remember being wakened in the morning, as I lay in my little trundle bed, by the sound of voices in the room. Now and then the talk would be interrupted by a sort of humming noise. It was the noise of a spinning wheel and the voices were those of the women who spun and carded the wool. The dust motes in the room sometimes danced in a ray of sunlight which shone through a high and narrow window, the only one by which the room was lighted. I often saw this dancing sunbeam in the early morning, for the house faced the east. In one corner of the room there was a great bed which had a coverlet, striped in brown and red, falling in folds to the very floor. There was a great brown cupboard or wardrobe standing with its back to the wall between the foot of the bed and the side of the room in which the window opened. All this comes back to me like a dim dream. And if I were asked to give the

simplest description of the faces of those poor young peasant women at their spinning wheels I could not do it, try
as I might.   For, although I had grown to be quite a lad
before they entirely disappeared out of my existence, I
can remember only their names from having heard them
spoken afterwards by members of my family. . . .

I remember certain vague sensations of those early
morning hours when I was first roused from sleep—for
example, the going and coming of the household, the
squawking of the geese in the courtyard, the crowing of
the cock, the rhythmic beats of the flail in the barn, and
other such familiar sounds, which made a kind of jumble
and none of which stands out with special distinctness. . . .

Here is a recollection a little more clear-cut.   The village had ordered some new church bells from the foundry,
two of the old ones having been carried off to make cannon
and the third having been cracked.   My mother wanted
to see the new bells which were standing on the floor of
the church awaiting consecration, before they were hoisted
into the tower. . . .   I remember how filled with awe
I was to find myself in a place so incredibly vast as the
church.   It seemed bigger than our barn.   The beauty of
the coloured windows and their settings of lead made a
great impression on me.   We saw all three bells which I
thought gigantic, for they were taller than I was.   Then—
and this is probably what fixed the whole scene so clearly
in my mind—Julie Lecacheux, my mother's servant-maid,
who held in her hand a great key—no doubt the key of the
church—ventured to strike the biggest of the bells.   I was
filled with admiration at the deep clang which followed.
I have never forgotten the blow of that key on that bell. . . .

I had a great uncle who was a priest.   He was fond of
me and took me everywhere with him.   I once went with
him to a house in which he was a frequent visitor.   Our
hostess was quite elderly and I recall her as a type of the

old-fashioned lady. She petted me and gave me some bread and honey and better still a peacock's feather. How good the honey was and how lovely the feather! I remember them yet.

This great uncle, my paternal grandfather's brother, had been a farm labourer and became a priest rather late in life. I believe he had, although I do not know exactly where, a small parish at the time of the Revolution. I know the Revolutionists persecuted him, for I have heard tell how they searched the house of my grandfather, where he was staying, in the most brutal fashion and tried to capture him. But he was very ingenious. He had contrived a hiding place close by his bedside into which he threw himself when his would-be captors came.

One day they came so suddenly that his bed was still warm when they reached it, and, although the family told them that he was not in the house, they cried: "Yes! Yes! He is somewhere here, for his bed is still warm, but he has managed to escape!" He could hear them talking. Beside themselves with anger they turned the house upside down before they left.

He used to celebrate Mass whenever he could in my father's house. I still have the leaden chalice which he used. After the Revolution he lived with his brother and filled the office of Vicar of the parish. Every morning he went to church to say Mass. After breakfast he used to work in the fields and frequently took me with him. In the fields he used to take off his cassock and work in his shirt sleeves and breeches. He was as strong as Hercules. There are still in existence, and they will last a long time yet, some high walls built of immense stones to support the terraces on a cultivated hillside. They look as if they had been built by a Cyclops. I have heard my grandmother and my father say that nobody helped him in laying even the heaviest stones, and there are some that would take five or six ordinary men, working with crowbars, to move.

He was a most kind-hearted man. He taught, for the love of God, the children of those villagers who were too poor to send their little ones to school. He taught them even a bit of Latin. This aroused the protest of his fellow priests in neighbouring villages who went so far as to lay a complaint against him with the Bishop. I once read, among some old papers, the first draft of a letter which he sent to the Bishop in his own defense and in which he said that he lived with his brother who was a peasant farmer; that he had found in the village some children who were deprived of any kind of schooling; that out of pity he had undertaken to teach them as well as he could; and he begged the Bishop, for Charity's sake, not to forbid him to teach these unfortunate youngsters to read. I have been told that the Bishop finally consented to let him go on. A generous permission, truly! . . . At his death I was about seven years old. It is very curious to recall the impressions which one has received in childhood and to take note of the indelible stamp which they leave upon the inmost character.

Young François had a good elementary education. He even studied some Latin, and his boyish acquaintance with the Bucolics and Georgics of Virgil and with the Bible influenced him all his life long. At school he was a great reader but not much of a mathematician. Although the so-called dreamy temperament of the artist disclosed itself in his childhood, he was by no means a milksop. Late in life he recalled, evidently with some pride, one of his schoolboyish adventures. The older boys used to egg on the younger ones to fight. Tom Browns of Rugby were apparently not confined to England. As Millet described it, the procedure was for an older boy to put a straw on the shoulder of a younger one and then say to still another youngster:

"I bet you don't dare to knock off that straw!" As no one wanted to be thought a coward the straw was immediately knocked off. It was a well-established tradition that nobody could tolerate an insult of this kind, and so the fight began in good earnest. The older boys cheered on the combatants until one or the other was vanquished. This procedure was followed in my case. I was the stronger and covered myself with glory. The boys who were backing me boasted of their choice. They went around saying: "Millet is only six and a half and he has knocked out a boy of more than seven!"

Millet's parents and doubtless Millet himself expected that he would be a farmer. But he spent all his leisure time in making untaught sketches of the people and scenes about him, and his father had the good sense to determine that his manifest talent ought to be cultivated. The boy was sent to Cherbourg to study with a local painter who had some local reputation. On his father's sudden death the young art student went back to Gruchy and tried to carry on the farm, but his grandmother and mother, both strong and wise women, saw that he was out of place and sent him back to his art studies. At the age of twenty-two he went to Paris to seek his fortune. The story of his life in Paris is pathetic in the extreme. He and his young wife suffered acutely from the actual physical deprivations of poverty. His wife, a delicate creature, died. Perhaps her death was hastened by the hardships which they shared in common. Millet was overwhelmed and went back to Normandy. There he again married a young peasant woman of remarkable personality who for thirty years proved to be his best friend. "Few but his most intimate friends," says Julia Cartwright, "knew how much he depended upon her sympathy and support, and the world is perhaps hardly yet aware how much it owes to Catherine Millet." With his new bride Millet courageously returned to Paris to begin the struggle over again. The popular taste for pictures in Paris in those days was at a low ebb. It was either formal and classical or frivolous. Millet's love for naturalism found no sympathy either in the professional ateliers, among the dealers, or in the public exhibitions. He had tried working in the studio of Delaroche but gave it up. What kept him going was his study of the great masters in the Louvre:

The sweetness, sanctity and ardour of the Primitives won my admiration. The skill and beauty of the Italian masters captivated me. There were moments when I felt as if I were pierced by the arrows of St. Sebastian when I looked at the canvases of Andrea Mantegna. The masters of that school have an incomparable and magnetic power. You share in the joys and sorrows which overwhelm them. But when I saw that drawing of Michelangelo's of a man in a swoon it was a veritable revelation. The relaxed muscles, the varying surfaces, the modelling of a body overcome with physical suffering, filled me with a complexity of feelings. Like him I felt the pangs of death. I had compassion on him. I suffered with the pain of his body and his limbs. I saw for the first time that it was possible to personify in a single figure the happiness and the misery of humanity. It was Michelangelo! To say that is to say everything. I had seen some inferior engravings of his work at Cherbourg, but here I entered into the spirit and heard the very voice of him who has so greatly influenced my whole life.

It was this experience combined with the ineffaceable impressions of his peasant boyhood that led to Millet's determination to devote himself to the portrayal of the farm labourer. But his resolution was carried out only with the greatest difficulty. The French Revolution had removed some of the shackles of the peasant but had not raised him in the estimation of what is called "society." Some of his farm pictures painted in this period of struggle in Paris, although now famous, were then ignored. To get bread for himself and his wife he tried to satisfy the current taste by producing pictures of the nude—sound, wholesome, and charming—but still they were nudes.   A little incident changed his course and led to his removal to Barbizon. Sensier tells the story:

Here is what produced this radical change. One evening, standing before the shop window of a dealer named Deforge, he noticed two young men looking at one of his pictures entitled "The Bathers." One said to the other, "Who painted that picture, do you know?" "Yes," replied his companion, "it is a man named Millet who does nothing but naked women." These words wounded him to the heart. It seemed as if he were condemned for life to be a painter of the nude, and his self-respect rose in rebellion. Going home he told his wife what had happened. "If you are willing," he said, "I will never paint another picture of this kind. You and I will have a hard time but I shall be free and can devote myself to the purpose which has been in my mind for a long time." His wife readily assented: "By all means follow your bent." From that time on Millet, liberated as it were from a kind of slavery, entered resolutely upon his career as a painter of peasant life in the fields.

With less than two thousand francs, part of which he loaned to his friend Jacque (who afterward became a highly esteemed painter of sheep and fowls) Millet and his family with Jacque and his family emigrated in a diligence to Barbizon on the edge of the forest of Fontainebleau.

Barbizon was thus destined to become the centre of a new movement in French art, and hence in the art of the world. Here Millet lived in quiet happiness for twenty-five years. His tastes were simple and his slowly won recognition brought him in enough money to provide for his modest wants. He would have been the most astonished of men if he could have foreseen the immense prices paid for his work after his death. The most famous of his pictures—but to my mind by no means the most beautiful or most interesting— the Angelus, was contentedly sold by Millet for $500, although the artist, so Sensier tells us, had a special affection for it. When it was bought a few years later by the well-known Paris dealer, Durand-Ruel for $6,000, Millet regarded the price as foolishly extravagant. What would he have thought if he could have witnessed the furor which the Angelus created in New York in 1889, when it was sold for more than $100,000 and the newspapers gave to the event almost as much space as they do to a prize fight! The picture was finally retrieved, at a cost of $150,000 by a French enthusiast, and it now rests in the country of its birth. The man whose work was thus to arouse unheard-of financial competition had to content himself with the strictest economy. One of my prized possessions is a leaf from one of Millet's sketch blocks. He had filled it with hasty sketches of figures drawn in his characteristic style and then, in order not to waste an inch of paper, had turned it upside down and sketched other figures in the open spaces left when the first set of sketches was completed. Even the walls of his little studio at Barbizon were used for sketching purposes. Thus is graphically recorded the simplicity and economy with which he worked.

Millet's life at Barbizon was a happy if simple one. He was devoted to his family, and although reserved and not at all gregarious, had a few devoted and congenial friends. Among the more intimate of them were Théodore Rousseau, the great landscapist, and Barye the great animal sculptor. It is pleasant to think that one or two Americans were gladly admitted by him to this intimate circle. He once said that the American painter, William Morris Hunt, who was both his pupil and his patron, was one of the best friends that he had ever had. Among this group of friends Sensier was, so to speak, his manager, attended to all his finances, and arranged many of his commissions and his exhibitions, and, as Millet expressed it, was a constant source of help, encouragement, and sympathy. Although far from extravagant and highly honourable in money matters, Millet had no head for business and was constantly pressed for funds. The financial side of his profession was the only one of its phases which gave him concern. An extract from one of his letters to Sensier is a fair example of the straits for money in which he found himself:

I am about to ask you something. Do me the favour, if you can, of sending me some cash—at least fifty francs and as much more as is convenient. I will repay you with the proceeds of the first canvas that I deliver,—Monsieur A., the Hollander and perhaps fifty others are possible purchasers. I was counting, when I perceived my funds running low, on devoting a day or two to making drawings for those two gentlemen; but severe headaches prevented and the bottom of my purse is already visible. If you can let me have the money please send it at once, *at once!* have just two francs left. Doubtless you will say that I ought not to have waited so long; but day before yesterday I was ill and flat on my back all day long, and yesterday the visit of the patron of whom I have spoken to you kept me from doing anything.

Sensier apologizes for printing this letter but says that he does so since Millet's very poverty ought to enhance our admiration for him because of the dignity and serenity with which he faced the hardships of his life, not allowing them in the slightest degree to disturb his perseverance and his devotion to his art.

Millet was a man of domestic tastes and found all the resource he required, outside of his art, in reading and in the quiet associations of family life. Virgil and the Bible were his favourite books—he called the Psalms his breviary—but he also read with enthusiasm Shakespeare, Milton, Burns, Theocritus, Emerson, and Channing, probably having been introduced to the last two by William Morris Hunt; he even undertook the study of Italian in order to read Dante. His tenderness for children appears in more than one of his letters. When Sensier lost a much-loved daughter Millet wrote:

I have just heard the news. Rousseau and I are coming to you at once. Take courage if you can.

A well-known French journalist, says Julia Cartwright, who visited Millet in Barbizon was much impressed with the cheerfulness of the patriarchal household. "Often Millet read aloud while his wife and daughters sewed, or else, if the evening was fine, the whole party took a ramble in the forest, singing and talking as they went."

I have been struck with the fact that four of the creative geniuses discussed in this book struggled with the handicap of ill-health which would have thrown less strong characters out of the race. Beethoven had his deafness; Darwin his chronic gastritis; Pasteur his paralysis; and Millet was no less a sufferer, for cruel and undiagnosed headaches, which no doctors seemed to be able to help, interrupted his working hours for the last twenty years of his life. He often had to take to his bed for two or three days at a time in agony. On one occasion he wrote to Sensier:

Headaches, constant headaches! Tell me how the Minister of Fine Arts has taken my appeal for a payment on account [he was expecting to paint a picture for the Government] for I am forced, like the Psalmist, to look to someone *unde veniet auxilium mihi*.

Sensier goes on to say that Millet at this time was so depressed by his physical sufferings that he had vague thoughts of putting an end to it all. He once gave Sensier a quite beautifully done sketch in black chalk of a painter lying dead at the foot of his easel, with his wife standing by the body in terrified grief. But Millet was too strong a character to yield to these morbid fancies. He remarked to Sensier one day, as though he were talking to himself: "Suicide is the act of a dishonourable man. What about his wife and children? A fine inheritance for them!" And then he added:

"Come, let's go out and see the sunset; it will cheer me up!"

In all these experiences of depression and hardship Millet's wife was his "guardian angel." Many people to-day appear to regard marriage as a more or less unimportant relationship that may be contracted or broken in the most light-hearted fashion. Biographical annals, however, are full of evidence that marriage successfully makes or irretrievably breaks the careers of the contracting parties. In Millet's case, as in the case of Darwin and of Pasteur, marriage proved to be an indispensable factor of his career. What these three men might have accomplished without the partnership of their wives is hardly worth speculation. Madame Millet survived her husband nearly twenty years and was comforted by his steadily growing celebrity. Her grave, says Julia Cartwright, is "by the side of the husband whose work she had helped so nobly during his lifetime and whose glory is her best reward."

Such a biographical sketch as that attempted here is not the place for critical judgments, even if I were competent to express them. But I may perhaps be permitted to say that such of his paintings as I have seen are not as appealing as his etchings and drawings. His colour is too often muddy and heavy. Is it not the human-istic poetry and imagination of his pictures rather than their technique—aside, that is, from his work in line, which is beautiful in form and composition—that gives him his preëminent place among artists? He painted not the heroic but the natural man. He was the Abraham Lincoln of artists and, like Lincoln, was suspected by the conventionalists of being an agitator. Bitterly hostile critics denounced his pictures of peasant life as an attempt to stir up another revolution. Millet's answer was this:

My programme is work, for man was designed for labour. "Thou shalt live by the sweat of thy brow," was written centuries ago and the immutable destiny of man will never change. What each man has to do is to try to progress in his profession, to strive for constant improvement so as to become effective and skillful in whatever career he has chosen and to attain superiority by the cultivation of his natural gifts and by his devotion to work. That is the path I have laid out for myself. All the rest is mere dreaming or speculation.

When the startling picture Death and the Woodcutter was refused admittance to the Salon of 1859, Millet said to his friend Sensier:

They think they can make me yield and can force me to paint drawing-room pictures. All right, I say No! A peasant I was born, a peasant I will die. I shall say what

I think and portray things as I see them, and mean to stand my ground without retreating a footstep.

There is a somewhat rare book in which W. E. Henley, the English poet, has gathered together twenty etchings and woodcuts by Millet which are all concerned with labour on the farm: Woman Carding Wool, Starting for Work, The Gleaners, The Spaders, The Shepherdess Knitting, The Manure Worker, Churning, Sewing, The Seated Shepherdess, A Woman at the Well, Mowing, Raking Straw, Binding Hay, Reaping, Threshing with a Flail, Woman Shearing Sheep, Woman Pulling Flax, Woman Crushing Flax, Man Cutting Fagots, Woman Spinning. No one can look at this collection of homely, everyday farm scenes without being struck by the fact that Millet was a naturalist. Romance did not interest him. He saw man, as he said, earning his bread by the sweat of his brow and was not dismayed. Moreover, the superb bodily action and the play of the muscles of the worker, the curves of the human form, the force, the energy, and the grace of motion all appealed to the eye of the artist in him. The Man with the Hoe did not seem to him the bestial, degenerate, depressing creature that he has seemed to be to one of our contemporary American poets. Sen-

TWELVE·   LOUIS PASTEUR

THE PHILANTHROPIST

BORN 1822—DIED 1895

CHEMISTRY is the basic science of modern civilization. It underlies industry, home life, agriculture, the manufacture and preservation of food, and the health of the individual and the community. A large portion of the human race would still be living like Hottentots or Esquimaux if it were not for the researches and discoveries of chemists.

There is another science that underlies even the laboratory, that is still more basic than synthetic-organic chemistry. It is philanthropy, which might be called psychological chemistry—the science of the reactions of human qualities on the individual and the community. Ignorance in handling and combining human qualities leads to acidity in the home, to boiling over and explosions in industry, and to lack of cohesion and tensile strength in government.

It must be a source of gratification to all scientists that some of the greatest physical

ble, he was overjoyed. In few thinkers of history has the two-sided nature of man—brain and soul, mind and spirit—been so distinguishable and yet so interlaced. Some passages selected at random from his writings and addresses by Sacha Guitry for his extraordinary play entitled "Pasteur" confirm this assertion:

Let not science be troubled by the effect of its discoveries upon theoretical philosophy. . . . So much the worse for those whose philosophical or political ideas are disturbed by my studies. In each of us there are two men,— the man of learning who wishes to educate himself by gaining a knowledge of nature and who discards all preconceived notions . . . and then the man of feeling, of faith and of doubt, the man who grieves for the children he has lost and cannot prove, alas! that he will see them again, but who believes and hopes for immortality, who does not want to die like a microbe, who says to himself that there is a mysterious power within him which will give him another form of existence. The two domains are distinct and maledictions on him who would encroach upon the rights of either in the present imperfect state of human knowledge!

Science in our century is the mother of national prosperity and the living source of all progress. Of course politics with its tiresome daily debates seems to be our guide, but politics is a will-o'-the-wisp. Our real guide is found in the discoveries of science and in our application of them.

I do not think I have ever come in contact with a student without saying to him: "Work and keep on working! Work gives the only lasting pleasure in life and is the only source of real profit to the individual and to the nation. Whatever career you adopt, set a high mark for yourself. Familiarize yourself with great men and great deeds,"—*ayez le culte des grands hommes et des grands choses.*

Speaking once to the undergraduates of the college at Arbois he said that whatever success he had achieved was due solely "to unremitting work and to no special gift or talent save that perhaps of perseverance united with an instinctive leaning towards all that is fine and noble." The similarity between this personal estimate and the self-analysis of Darwin is striking. He who ventures to say that Pasteur's spiritual achievements were as admirable as his scientific discoveries will not be far astray. At all events, one cannot read his life without feeling, as one feels in reading the life of his distinguished fellow countryman and fellow scientist, Fabre, the beauty of simplicity, sincerity, patience, determination, devotion to truth, and faith in a mysterious but divine purpose in the universe.

Pasteur's parents were plain people but had intelligence and character. His father was a tanner by trade, served as a soldier in the Napoleonic wars of 1812-14, was promoted to be sergeant major, and received for personal bravery the cross of the Legion of Honour. His mother's family were gardeners. The Napoleonic soldier, having returned to his tannery

The biography of Pasteur is, as one of his pupils has aptly said, the history of a mind. It is questionable if in the development of any other scientist there may be so clearly seen the ramifications of the roots and branches of the intellect. His first success was in the chemistry of mineralogy, and he was elected to the Academy of Science in Paris in the section of mineralogy. He became an expert in crystallography and in the use of the delicate goniometer. Not long before his student days the chemist Dumas had stated before the Academy of Science the law of molecular substitution: "Chlorine possesses the peculiar power of seizing upon hydrogen in certain substances and of replacing it atom by atom." This chemical law Pasteur investigated with ardour. The gift which he had for simplifying complicated scientific theories is exemplified by the simile he once employed in explaining this law. Chemical substances, he said, are like "buildings made of molecules in which one element may be substituted for another without changing the structure of the building, exactly as one might substitute stone for stone in a monument without altering its general form." His boldness as an investigator impressed his colleagues, but it did not tempt him to make hasty and erroneous conclusions. "It may be so," he was in the habit of saying, "but let us look a little further into the subject."

From inorganic chemistry, Pasteur turned to organic chemistry and studied, in pursuance of the germ theory, which he afterward established, the diseases of silkworms, of sheep and poultry, and of what might also be said to be the diseases of beer and wine. His purpose in this was to help the industries of his country. From the study of epidemics among farm animals he turned to the investigation of human diseases. His employment of inoculation to cure the little Alsatian boy, Joseph Meister, of hydrophobia, is a romance in itself to which I shall refer again.

The long process by which Pasteur worked out the theory of antitoxins, and applied it in fighting the microbian diseases of plant and animal life, is highly technical. To attempt an accurate description of it in such a biographical sketch as this would be out of place. But it may be said that what he discovered was that he could produce a weak or attenuated serum or culture of a germ or microbe, and that inoculation with this weak vaccine would make the plant or animal immune to the more virulent form of the microbe. Still further, he found that if a living being were already stricken with a virulent germ disease, inoculation with the attenuated culture of the germ would afford resistance to the disease and in a large percentage of cases effect a cure. The outstanding results on modern life of his discoveries are the prevention of typhoid by preinoculation and the cure of diphtheria and hydrophobia by post-inoculation.

Pasteur did not achieve his goal without a struggle. He had to overcome jealousy, incredulity, and slander. In one instance, he was nearly involved in a duel with a fellow member of the Academy of Sciences. Although he was simple and direct in his methods, his final success was dramatic in the extreme. Take the story of his victory over anthrax, for example.

Anthrax, or splenic fever (so-called because of the enlarged spleens of the victims), was a perfect plague in Europe. Horses, cows, oxen, sheep, and even shepherds, cowherds, and hostlers succumbed to the dread disease. Pasteur first satisfied himself that it was caused by a communicable germ which he isolated in his laboratory. He found, by a study of earthworms, that they carried these germs from the bodies of dead and buried animals to the surface grass and that healthy animals contracted the disease when they were pastured on this grass. He further convinced himself than an attenuated serum would weaken or destroy the power of the fatal germ. His pronouncements were greeted with scepticism or ridicule, but he was now ready for a practical demonstration.

The Agricultural Society of Melun, not far from Paris, placed a farm, known as Pouilly le Fort, at his disposal with sixty healthy sheep. He directed that twenty-five should be inoculated with attenuated anthrax serum, that a few days later these twenty-five and twenty-five of the unvaccinated sheep should receive a subcutaneous injection of a virulent anthrax culture, and that the remaining ten of the sixty should be kept for comparison. He predicted that the twenty-five unvaccinated sheep would perish, and that the twenty-five inoculated with the antitoxin would recover and be as sound as the ten reserved as a standard of comparison. The epoch-making test was carried out, in accordance with Pasteur's programme, in the presence of a distinguished company of agriculturists, physicians, chemists, and veterinary surgeons. It was a complete success. Pasteur's predictions were fulfilled to the letter. His son-in-law thus describes the dénouement:

Early in June Messrs. Chamberland and Roux [Pasteur s pupils and assistants] went back to Pouilly le Fort to examine the condition of the inoculated sheep. . . .

All the unvaccinated animals were getting worse and worse. They were all gasping for breath. The heaving of their flanks was now and then broken by groans. When they attempted to walk they could only take a few steps reeling and tottering. . . . Pasteur's anxiety was great when Messrs. Chamberland and Roux returned and made their report. Having carefully worked out his bold programme without neglecting a single detail, he had been imperturbable in making his experiment on these sheep whose life or death would decide whether he had made an immortal discovery or a hopeless failure. Now, by a sudden reaction, he was filled with doubt and distress. . . . His emotional nature, so strangely allied to his fighting instinct, was in control. For a little while his faith failed him and he feared that his experiments were about to betray him. He passed a sleepless night. . . . When, the next day, he arrived at Pouilly le Fort, accompanied by his young assistants, a murmur growing into a burst of applause greeted him. Delegates from the Melun Agricultural Society and from various medical, sanitary, and veterinary organizations, reporters, small farmers, whom the eulogies and attacks of the newspapers had confused and did not know whether they ought to honour a great discoverer or denounce a charlatan,—all these were there. The bodies of twenty-two unvaccinated animals lay side by side in death; two other sheep were at their last gasp. [A third died that night.] All showed the characteristic signs of the deadly anthrax. The twenty-five vaccinated sheep were perfectly sound and well. Pasteur's triumph was complete. The veterinary surgeons, who had been the most sceptical, were now convinced and asked nothing better than to become Pasteur's disciples.

The tide had turned, and Pasteur, who had formerly been the sufferer from widespread

ironical criticism, was now showered with honours. Huxley said that his discovery saved
France in money alone an amount sufficient to
make up the entire indemnity which she paid
Germany after the Franco-Prussian War.

Meanwhile, even during his anxious waiting
for the results of his anthrax test, Pasteur went
on with his laboratory investigations of hydrophobia. When warned that he was overwork-
ing, he answered: "I should feel as if I were a
thief if I were to let a day go by without working." Those antivivisectionists who have not
been convinced of their error by the statistics of
human lives saved and animal suffering allevi-
ated through Pasteur's experimentation, ought
at least to be softened in their attitude toward
him by his hatred of cruelty. His laboratory
assistant, Dr. Roux, pictures his solicitude for
the welfare of the dogs that were the subjects
of his tests.

He could take part without much reluctance in a simple
operation, a subcutaneous inoculation, for instance, but
even then, if the animal yelped a little, he was filled with
pity and tried to soothe the victim with encouraging and
comforting words that would have been laughable if they
had not been so pathetic. The very thought of perforating
the skull of a dog was repellent to him. He ardently
wanted to complete his experiments and yet he hesitated
to proceed. One day I trephined a dog when he was

absent. The following morning when I was describing the ease with which the intercranial inoculation had been accomplished, he began pitying the dog. "Poor fellow! His brain is probably injured. I suppose he is paralyzed." Saying nothing I went into the basement, found the dog and brought him up into the laboratory. Pasteur was not especially fond of dogs, but when he saw this one running about, full of life, investigating every corner of the room, he was overjoyed and showered the poor beast with words of commendation. He was always deeply grateful to this particular dog for having undergone the operation of trepanning so successfully and for having thus removed his hesitancy to perform similar operations in the future.

Pasteur thus carried on his investigation of rabies or hydrophobia, called by Sir Henry Roscoe, the English chemist, "the most horrible of all diseases"—horrible because, until Pasteur's discoveries, there was apparently no cure for it and no means of alleviating its monstrous agonies.

One of Pasteur's childish recollections [says his son-in-law] was the state of terror into which the people of the Jura region were thrown by a mad wolf that bit scores of animals and humans. He had seen the wounds of one of these victims, a citizen of Arbois by the name of Nicole, cauterized with a red-hot iron in a blacksmith shop not far from his father's house. Persons bitten on the hands and face died of hydrophobia, some of them in atrocious suffering. In three villages alone there were eight victims. Nicole was the only one saved. For years throughout that region people talked about the fearful days of the mad wolf.

Pasteur proceeded as he did in the case of anthrax. He made an attenuated culture of the medulla oblongata of dogs attacked by rabies, and found that it was a prophylactic. Writing to the Emperor of Brazil in 1884 he said:

I have not yet dared to experiment on men in spite of my confidence in the result and of the numerous opportunities which have come in my way. I am afraid that a failure might compromise ultimate success. I want first to be assured by a large number of experiments on animals. So far things are going very well. I have already a number of examples of dogs who have resisted rabietic infection. I take two dogs and cause them to be bitten by a mad dog. I vaccinate one and do nothing to the other. The unvaccinated dog dies of rabies; the vaccinated dog does not contract the disease. But even when I have multiplied these examples of prophylaxis of hydrophobia in dogs I am afraid my hand would tremble if I tried the experiment on a man.

He said the same things again in writing to a French friend:

I have demonstrated this year that by vaccination it is possible to give dogs the power of resistance to rabies when they have been bitten by mad dogs. I have not yet, however, dared to try this remedy on men. But the hour for attempting the remedy in the case of a human being cannot long be postponed. I am almost inclined to start with myself, that is to say, to inoculate myself with rabies and then counteract the effects by vaccination, for I am beginning to have faith in myself and to be sure of the results.

The hour was not long postponed nor did Pasteur have to try the remedy on his own person. A few months later, in 1885, a mother from an Alsatian village brought her boy into his laboratory, little Joseph Meister, nine years old. He had been savagely bitten by a mad dog, and the local doctor had advised the mother to take the boy to Paris where there was a famous man who, although not a physician, could tell her better than any physician whether anything could be done to save the child from a horrible death. Nothing had been done for the boy except to wash his wounds with carbolic acid. Pasteur was deeply moved. He made the boy and his mother comfortable and then consulted a colleague, who was a specialist in nervous diseases, as to whether he should venture upon inoculation. It was his colleague's opinion that Pasteur's successful experiments with dogs justified him in inoculating the boy. It could do no harm; it might do good. Two other experts who were consulted gave the same advice, and the boy was inoculated twelve times with the prophylactic serum. He completely recovered, and his cure led to the founding of the Pasteur Institute, where thousands of cases have been successfully treated since, the mortality being reduced to an almost negligible percentage.

Subscriptions for the Pasteur Institute poured in from all over the world, and Pasteur was much touched when he found Joseph Meister's name on the list of subscribers. Those who wish to know how the case of Joseph Meister affected the hearts of the French people will be interested to read Sacha Guitry's play, in which the main facts of the story are given, although embroidered with all the imaginative detail of a gifted dramatist.

The effect of Pasteur's pathological researches afford an interesting study in psychology. It is a frightful and faith-shaking thing to think of a power in nature which first makes the hideous anthrax bacterides that swim through the blood like tangled microscopic snakes, and then establishes an antitoxic law by which their deadly battening may be frustrated. Why is it? Why create a microbe and then create a law for its destruction? This inferno of doom which Pasteur, most clear-eyed of mortals, distinctly saw might have made him, some would think, a hopeless pessimist. But this is what he said in his address when he was received into the *Académie française:*

What is beyond? Man, driven by an irresistible force, never ceases to ask "What is beyond?" Even if he tries to content himself with one moment of finite time or one spot of finite space he no sooner becomes familiar with it than the persistent question recurs and he cannot suppress the outcry of his longing to know. It is no use to tell him that beyond is limitless space and limitless time. No one can comprehend those terms. He who admits the existence of the Infinite—and no one can escape it—puts into his admission more of the supernatural than can be found in all the miracles of the various religions of mankind; for the conception of infinity has the double quality of being axiomatic and incomprehensible. When this conception grips our understanding, we can only prostrate ourselves. . . . I see everywhere in the world the inescapable expression of the Infinite. As long as the mystery of infinity weighs upon the mind of man, so long will temples be built for the worship of the Infinite, whether the worshipped Deity is called Brahma, Allah, Jehovah, or Jesus. And upon the mosaic pavement of those temples you will find men kneeling, prostrate, overwhelmed by the thought of the infinite.

Pasteur enjoyed a steadily growing success and recognition, although the traditionalists fought him tooth and nail. He was given the honourary degree of doctor of medicine by the University of Bonn in 1868; received the grand cross of the Legion of Honour in 1881; and was in 1882 elected to the French Academy, the greatest honour that can be conferred upon a French intellectual. His seventieth birthday was observed by an international celebration at which Lister, the British scientist, in a public apostrophe to Pasteur said:

You have raised the veil which for centuries has covered infectious diseases; you have discovered and demonstrated their microbian nature.

Tyndall wrote to him:

For the first time in the history of science we have a right to the sure and certain hope that, so far as epidemic diseases are concerned, medicine will soon be freed from quackery and placed upon a scientific basis; when that great day comes humanity, I believe, will recognize that a large part of its gratitude is due to you.

And Darwin added his testimony:

I was struck with infinite admiration at his work.

This great summit, however, had not been reached without mental and physical suffering. In 1868, when he was forty-six years old, Pasteur had a stroke of paralysis. In 1888, another temporarily paralyzed his tongue. For nearly thirty years after the first stroke his left leg dragged a little. But it was during that thirty years that his greatest contributions to the welfare of mankind were made. The Franco-Prussian War was a great blow to him, for he had dreamed of the fraternity of mankind based on scientific knowledge. The barbarity of the Prussians in their invasion of Paris when they destroyed the laboratory of one of his colleagues, breaking the glass tubes of barometers and thermometers, knocking scales and other instruments out of shape with hammers, and burning to ashes the notes and records and manuscripts of ten years' work, so incensed him that he returned to the University of Bonn his medical diploma, with a dignified note of protest. In his early life he worked with inadequate laboratory equipment. The indifference of the French Government and even of the Department of Education was disheartening. His first laboratory at the École Normale was in an almost uninhabitable attic. His friend and associate, the chemist Laurent, died at fifty-three of a disease contracted from working in a pseudo-laboratory installed in an unsanitary cellar. Pasteur made constant protests against the indifference of the authorities to scientific research. He once said, in a moment of discouragement: "For more than twenty years I have been suffering from the contempt which France has for great intellectual labour." But these trials never destroyed his human kindness. He practised, as he preached to his students, the cult of great men. He once said:

From the records of men whose lives have been marked by rays of shining light let us faithfully preserve every word, every act which can help posterity to understand and appreciate the spiritual sources of their power.

This I take as the justification of my biographical sketch. His faith in the divine spark which glows even through the darkness of human selfishness and misery is recorded in a few trenchant words which may be said to have been his creed:

> I believe without a shadow of doubt that science and peace will finally triumph over ignorance and war and that the nations of the earth will ultimately agree not to destroy but to build up.

It is illustrative of Pasteur's modern point of view that he expressed this belief a generation before the World War gave birth to the League of Nations.

Pasteur, like Darwin, was fortunate in the happiness of his family life. His domestic relations were an important factor in his scientific career. It has already been seen what were his associations with his father, mother, and sister in his boyhood and youth. At the age of twenty-six he was a young professor at the College of Strasburg. There he met the family of the new rector of that institution whose name was Laurent and fell in love with his daughter. The dreadful year which has taken her from us. If she had lived she would have been a companion and friend for her mother and me. But forgive me, my dear father, for speaking of these sad memories. She is happy. Let us fix our minds on those who are left and do everything we can to defend them from the sorrows of life.

Pasteur died literally in the trenches during his warfare on hydrophobia. A branch of his Paris laboratory had been established in the park of the old château of Villeneuve l'Étang near St. Cloud. When his strength began to fail during the last summer of his life, he was taken out to this laboratory, where his bedroom opened upon the lawn and the fine old shade trees of the park. His son-in-law gives an affecting account of the last weeks of his life:

Seated on the terrace of the old château of Villeneuve l'Étang, under the shade of a group of pines and purple beeches, he listened happily to his wife and daughter who read aloud to him. They had that brave faculty of smiling which women are able to display even when suffering anguish of heart. Biographies greatly interested him as they always had in the past. In those days, even after a long period of peace, Frenchmen liked to hear again the distant echo of the cannons of the First Empire. The reading world was absorbed in the reminiscences, the letters, the stories of war. Pasteur was never wearied by these recollections. They often recalled the patriotic enthusiasm of his youth. But "*la gloire*" no longer seemed to him what it did in earlier years. The real leaders, he now believed, were not the military conquerors but the servants of humanity. After pages full of thrilling deeds of war, he turned with satisfaction to the life of that great and good man, St. Vincent de Paul. Pasteur loved this son of peasant parents who, in an epoch of pride in ancestry, was never ashamed of his humble birth; this tutor of a future cardinal whose real desire was to be the comforter of galley slaves; this priest who was the spiritual father of foundlings and who organized philanthropy in a great system of benevolence for laymen and ecclesiastics.

These happy surroundings, while they soothed the dying chemist, could not save him. His life was ended by a third and final stroke of paralysis on the 28th of September, 1895, "one of his hands in the hand of his wife, the other holding a crucifix."

The name of this great modernist has become a household word, for the verb "to pasteurize" is known in every home enlivened by the voices of children. Let us hope that, in fulfillment of his dream, the microbes of political and racial hatred may finally be pasteurized out of international relations by the warmth of human kindness. If this can ever be accomplished it might well be called the greatest psychochemical reaction of history.

POSTSCRIPTUM

WHATEVER may be the fate of this book I have been repaid for the labour of writing it—perhaps compiling it might be a more accurate phrase—by the pleasure of living for several years in association with the men whose lives and personalities I have endeavoured to portray. The work has been done in such hours of leisure as could be obtained in the midst of more active and prosaic duties. One of its satisfactions is that it has led to far more reading than writing. It is impossible to read the words of such a group of twelve men, and the words about them written by their personal friends or biographers, without feeling that one has lived with them. I have enjoyed them all, respect them all, and am grateful to them all for what they have done for me—with one possible exception. For Voltaire my feeling is somewhat akin to pity, although his wit and humanitarianism command my admiration.

Of the twelve there are four with whom I should especially like to have been thrown on terms of personal intimacy. I wish I might have pitched quoits in the Barbecue Club with John Marshall; or have heard the choir of King's Chapel and walked in the garden of "Down House" in company with Charles Darwin; or have watched Millet paint in his village studio at Barbizon, while I listened to his stories of the Normandy peasants; or dined with Pasteur at his house in Arbois when he twirled his cherries, one by one, in his glass of water to wash off the microbes and then drank the water in his absent-minded enthusiasm over the recovery of little Joseph Meister. I should have felt overwhelmed by St. Francis's divine goodness and by Emerson's transcendental intellect, but I think that I should have understood Marshall and Millet, Darwin and Pasteur, and that they would, perhaps, have understood me.

THE END

4194